Set For Life

Quantity discounts are available on bulk orders.
Contact info@TAGPublishers.com for more information.

TAG Publishing, LLC
2618 S. Lipscomb
Amarillo, TX 79109
www.TAGPublishers.com
Office (806) 373-0114
Fax (806) 373-4004
info@TAGPublishers.com

ISBN: 978-1-59930-407-6

First Edition

Copyright © 2012 John Svalina

All rights reserved. No part of this book may be reproduced in any form without prior written permission from the publisher. The opinions and conclusions drawn in this book are solely those of the author. The author and the publisher bear no liability in connection with the use of the ideas presented.

Set For Life
Financial Peace of Mind Made Easy

John Svalina

I would like to dedicate this book to two people in my life who have been shining examples of what can be achieved through hard work, dedication and love, my parents Ivica and Marica Svalina. To say that they have my unending gratitude does not even come close to expressing my love for their example of how to live life. I will strive my entire life to be the same kind of example to my children and can only hope to achieve as good a result. I love you Mom & Dad. XO

About the Author

John Svalina is an award winning financial professional with seventeen years of success providing high net worth business owners, professionals and retirees with ongoing wealth management planning, advice and service for all of their wealth management needs. Since 2002, John has been a Vice President and Portfolio Manager with the Hickey & Svalina Wealth Management Group at a major Canadian financial institution. The Hickey & Svalina Wealth Management Group manages over $430 million in client assets and is the recipient of several awards of distinction. John focuses on creating a strong long term relationship with his clients and is passionate about ensuring their financial dreams become reality. John was born in Sudbury Ontario where he currently resides with his wife Tina and their children Johnny and Anna.

Contents

Foreword..11

Chapter 1
The Nest Egg Illusion..13

Chapter 2
Money Matters..29

Chapter 3
The Right Fit..45

Chapter 4
You are HERE..59

Chapter 5
Retirement is Not the End!..................................77

Chapter 6
Handing Down the Wealth..................................95

Chapter 7
Estate Planning..105

Chapter 8
Put Your Money Where Your Heart Is.............119

Chapter 9
Lost and Stolen Nest Eggs.................................135

Chapter 10
The Real Goal is Peace of Mind........................147

Glossary..159

FOREWORD

I have been very impressed with John Svalina's passion for assisting families in understanding the sometimes complex world of wealth management. As an industry leading, award winning financial professional, John has helped high net worth, and ultra high net worth, families ensure their fortunes will continue to grow for generations to come and now, for the first time, he opens up and shares some of his common-sense wealth strategies in this book. John's unique insight into the real reasons people don't plan for the future, allow him to uncover and address the issues that will allow his clients to move forward and live their dreams.

October 21, 2011 marked 50 years from the day I picked up Napoleon Hill's classic, *Think and Grow Rich*. I've been a serious student of the mind and have spent virtually all of my adult life studying human behavior: why we do the things we do and don't do some of the things we know will bring us better results. As John aptly points out, "Wealth isn't determined by investment performance, but by investor behavior." Our behavior creates our financial results (i.e. our bank account, our investment portfolio, etc.) and the only way we can change our results is to change our thinking. This book will help you change your thinking with respect to wealth management.

I know how important a role fear plays in many people's lives especially when it comes to money. This probably stems from the fact that, as a general rule, we're not taught anything about money and we're certainly not accustomed to openly discuss it. Money is really just an idea and each person has complete control over their ability to grow what they have and earn as much as they choose. Of course earning money is only half of the equation, effectively managing cash flow and investments is the other half. I'm a firm believer in seeking out sound advice in areas in which I'm not overly savvy.

The caveat I would add to this is to seek out advice from someone who has proven, by their results, that they know what they're doing. John Svalina's track record with respect to wealth management speaks for itself.

In his new book, *Set for Life*, John discusses the key elements for growing your wealth and then passing it on to the next generation. The foundation of his approach is family involvement and financial education, two things that most people don't even consider, but which are vital to real change.

In today's uncertain environment, financial literacy is more vital than ever to overcome the fear that can easily set in when our lives unexpectedly change. We all want to explore our dreams and live an abundant life but so many become complacent and just accept the status quo. Most people go after what they think they can achieve, as opposed to what they really want. As my mentor Earl Nightingale would say, "Most people think they want more money than they really do, and they settle for a lot less than they could get." Armed with the proper information, your financial goals are within your reach and it may be easier than you imagine. But, it does require your full participation.

John clarifies and clearly communicates the steps necessary for you to reach your financial goals. There is no reason to wait; all it takes is a decision – one clear decision – to set you on the path to financial peace of mind.

Bob Proctor
Bestselling Author of *You Were Born Rich*

Chapter 1

The Nest Egg Illusion

Chapter 1
The Nest Egg Illusion

Financial peace of mind is something that I think every single person strives for, or at least hopes for, in their life. Yet as we mature, our idea of financial peace changes and evolves. When we are young, we want to ensure our basic needs are provided for and that we build some type of foundation for the future.

As our families grow, our financial concerns grow as well and we strive to ensure that those concerns are well thought out and planned for. Later, as we think about our own mortality, we also may wish to ensure our legacy and to pass on the wealth we have accumulated in the most advantageous way to future generations.

No one wants to worry about outliving their money due to poor choices, lack of planning, or by falling victim to some elaborate investment scheme – but we also know those things happen every day to people we know or have heard about. It's not just the amount of money that we worry about, but what that money represents and that is our way of life, our safety and our future lifestyle options. We want to ensure we will not outlive our resources, lose more than we make on investments, and that our families will benefit from a lifetime of our hard work.

In my business I deal with a large number of high net worth people. They are millionaires or multi-millionaires, many with large financial interests both at home and abroad. It is interesting that although many of these people are incredibly intelligent and virtually all self-made, they have the same worries and concerns that everyone else has concerning their money. While they may have more of it, that doesn't mean they are experts on keeping it safe or knowing what steps to take to protect themselves. So they, just like everyone else, can find themselves lying awake at night worrying about their future.

Many of us are taught that we should save, save, save all our lives and build a nest egg and then all will be well. But guess what – that is an illusion. A pile of money is just that – a pile. You have to know what to do with it or it deteriorates. Developing and implementing sound financial strategies doesn't just magically happen, nor does the ability to earn money automatically give you the ability to keep it safe or invest it. I can't tell you how many people I meet on a daily basis that have earned their money, but then are worried sick about what to do next. This is the clearest indication that financial peace has nothing to do with the amount of money you have.

Human beings are emotional creatures – you have to accept that fact first before you can begin to understand why we behave the way we do where money is concerned. If it was purely a numbers game, then we'd simply work out the formulas and all would be well – but that isn't what happens. Every time the stock markets take a little bounce I see firsthand the panic, fear and uncertainty that arises in peoples' minds. Logic would say this instant reaction to a small hiccup in the market is unreasonable as we all know that the markets correct themselves on occasion but over time post respectable gains. But that is not what is going through your head as your eyes are glued to that stock ticker and you see your investments starting down what you perceive to be a slippery slope to oblivion.

Even if you know better in your head, your heart picks up paces and the next thing you know you are calling your broker in a panic.

This fear has nothing to do with the numbers on paper. This has to do with the threat (whether real or perceived) that your way of life and all that you have worked for is about to take a big hit. The 'what ifs' roll through your mind as you consider all the years of work that you have put in to getting where you are and it can become paralyzing, or worse, lead you to make some terrible decisions.

When I started to write this book, I decided to get down to the root cause of the problem and address it head on instead of dancing around it like the elephant in the room. So as you read you will notice that this isn't one of those books that says, "Do X, then Y and then Z and all will be well". In order to really understand yourself and your relationship with money, we have to examine it all and that means we will dust off those old experiences and events that created your mindset toward money and figure out what might help you move forward to feeling complete peace with your financial situation no matter how much you have.

As you think back on your relationship with money, the first things that usually come to mind are the important lessons we all learn about finances, some positive and some negative. In my case, I think back to what I learned from my parents and grandparents. My family originated from what is now Croatia. Both my grandmothers were housewives, as was the norm then, and my grandfathers were both farmers during the week and lumberjacks on the weekends. They worked very hard and everything they had came from their own effort. My parents as young people knew there was a better life to be had in North America and they wanted to experience those options and possibilities. In the 1960s my parents both immigrated to Canada separately then met and married.

My mother had a grade 6 education and was only 14 when she set foot on Canadian soil searching for the 'better life' her parents so wanted her to experience. My grandfather accompanied her to the train station to send her off and say goodbye. He left her with a loaf of bread, some lunch meat and a little pocket knife. He told her he loved her with all of his heart and if she wanted to come back that he would sell everything he had to get her home. When she arrived in Canada, she couldn't speak one word of English and her Aunt was the only person she knew. Like so many immigrants, all she had was a suitcase and a dream. My mom still has the little pocket knife her father gave her and to me it's a symbol of the ability of any person to strike out into the unknown and make their own way.

My father graduated from a trade school and was a diesel mechanic. After my parents married in August of 1970, my mom worked as a custodian at Cambrian College. Her shift was from 10:30 pm to 7 am - and she worked that shift for 18 years. She would arrive home from work and then get us ready and off to school each and every morning with a smile on her face and an unlimited supply of hugs and kisses before we got on the school bus. My dad often worked 12-15 hour days as a mechanic. I remember as a child, seeing my Dad's hands after working outside in the middle of winter on a broken down transport truck and trailer. They were always red and swollen.

I know how hard my parents had to work to earn a living yet I never once heard them complain. Growing up, we always had everything we needed and were always surrounded by love. I'm grateful for my wonderful childhood years and everything my parents taught me by example. Together, they worked around the clock to support and raise three children. This is the kind of work ethic and determination I grew up with and that had an effect on me as I started my own life. I understood that it was no small thing to earn a living, but it was possible if you worked hard.

The Debt Demon

When I started college, I worked the night shift in the summer months stocking shelves at the grocery store in our neighborhood to pay for school as I was determined to graduate with no debt (which I did). I also learned that I never wanted to work the night shift ever again! It was very difficult to get through many of those nights. I remember some nights sleeping on the bottom shelf behind rolls of toilet paper waiting for 8 am to come. I was a walking zombie most of the time. Even today, I often wonder how my mom managed to work night shift for 18 years and still always be there for us.

My first year in university, I received a pre-approved VISA card in the mail with a $2,000 credit limit. It was really exciting; I felt like I had a million dollars – and started spending that way. In less than a month I had that card maxed out. I don't remember what I purchased but I do know that I had nothing to show for it. I'm guessing it was probably a spring break bus trip to Florida along with various assorted purchases of beer, pizza and chicken wings. With all the other school related expenses that I was funding from working 20 hours a week part time at the grocery store, I had little discretionary income left. Panic soon set in as it does for many young people when they take on their first debt.

It took me almost a year to pay the credit card balance off. What really bothered me was that I had this seeming huge debt but nothing tangible to show for it. It was all spent on temporary indulgences and thrills that wore off almost immediately – and those thrills certainly didn't overcome the dread of opening the statement each month afterwards! I remember how much anxiety I felt and knew that I never wanted to feel that way again. It threatened my way of life and could have threatened my ability to complete my education and that idea was incomprehensible to me. I could have ruined my future.

I'm grateful that I learned my lesson while I was in school instead of in the real world, but many people don't. There are many individuals today living in mansions that are so heavily leveraged that they can't even breathe because one even relatively minor disaster would crush their house of cards and that is a very stressful, unhappy way to live.

Even though I had learned the lesson of too much debt, there were bigger and much more difficult lessons I needed to learn. Once out of college, I decided to try day trading. Many people were having great success with it at the time. I was living at home and my expenses were low and while day trading was a risk, I thought it was a great time to try it. I invested $7000 of savings in my efforts and before long I grew it to over $82,000. It was like a fortune to a kid who had worked the last few years stocking grocery store shelves just to get through school! I was so excited and very proud of myself to the point I really started to believe that I was actually a skilled day trader. I felt invincible! So I bet bigger and took on more risk. The next thing you know, I made two highly speculative trades on margin and that whole $82,000 was gone. Just gone. I was devastated. I thought the world was ending and was crushed to the point of being physically sick because I'd just lost more money than I'd ever had in my whole life.

I couldn't sleep and eventually had to take sleeping pills for the first time in my life just to get some rest. I was absolutely miserable. The good thing was that I was still living at home so I didn't make myself homeless or lose more than the money I'd invested. Just like my credit card experience, I looked at myself in the mirror and told myself that I never want to feel this way again. It was at that point that I knew I had to learn as much as I could about different investment strategies and then develop one that works for me. I took a particular interest in Warren Buffett's approach to investing because it was easy to understand and made sense. In 1993, I purchased shares in his company Berkshire Hathaway and still own them today. I hope to give them to my grandchildren one day. I eventually wrote my own Investment Policy Statement which continues to govern how I manage my family's investment portfolio. I no longer swing for the fences and believe wholeheartedly that most turtles do win the investment race.

Lessons Frame Our Perspective

These were just a few of the lessons in my life that framed how I view money and investing and each of us have our own experiences. The interesting thing is that sometimes we can let a negative experience shade our view of money and investing to the point we refuse to make decisions that will help us. Almost every person has some issues – either minor or major - with some part of money management. It might be in the area of debt, investing in stocks, their view of bonds, or even a bias against insurance! It is important to remember that nothing appears out of a void, so each of these ideas comes from somewhere. They may have come from how you were raised, the people you spend time around or experiences that you have had. All of these shape our perceptions and thus dictate how we make decisions about money.

How often have you heard someone say, "Oh, I'd never invest in rental property; that's a pit." Really? Some of the richest self-made people in the world made their fortune in real estate so you know that is not a valid statement. But it is still how we feel – not logic – that determines what actions we take. I've also talked to clients who will make statements like "Tech is dead, don't put my money in that!" or "I want my money in cash so I can get to it." The statements aren't logical or valid from an investment strategy standpoint, but they are valid from an emotional standpoint and in order to move forward, the reasons behind those feelings need to be discovered and addressed. This is the first step toward emotional discipline and it is vital to maximizing the growth of your money and protecting your assets in a sound way.

Emotional Discipline was one of the first lessons that really sank in for me. As a young person in the investment industry, I was aware that there are two sources of income: you at work and your money at work. I was fascinated with learning how to make my money work so I never had to work night shift again. I also learned that debt is money working against you.

When I first started as a money manager, I was obsessed with the idea of wealth accumulation. I thought my job was simply to make my client's money and so that's what I focused on. As I grew with my clients, I became more interested with providing solutions to their wealth preservation and transition needs as they went from one phase of life, or earning, to another. I asked them questions about their goals and dreams for their work and career, well-being, home, lifestyle and legacy. Some of the questions I still ask are:

- What are the most important issues that are facing you and your family right now?
- What are the specific goals or desires you have for you and your family?
- How and when will you move on from your current responsibilities at your job or business?
- What is the impact of being unable to continue what you're currently doing?
- What keeps you up at night?

- How will you protect your family's standard of living in the event of a birth, unexpected death or prolonged illness?
- What are you doing to protect your physical and emotional health?
- What's the significance of your home in your long-term plans?
- How do you measure success in your life?
- How will your life change in the next 5, 10, 15 years?
- How do you want to be remembered?

These are questions that I have asked myself over the years. Not one of these questions talks about how much money you have or how much you want. It's not about how much money you can make, but more about creating a peaceful, secure, happy life.

After years of study and practice, I know that to succeed as an investor, you need to incorporate several key actions into your strategy. I start with these as they help lay the foundation for your decision-making. They include:

Develop your own written Investment Policy Statement as the rule of engagement. My wife and I have our own for our family and this keeps us on track. It reminds us of what we want to accomplish and being able to see that big picture keeps the smaller issues in their proper perspective.

Our Investment Policy Statement clearly lays out our objectives but also includes things such as our planning horizon and risk tolerance.

These things are agreed up and allow us to select a mix of investments that will meet our stated objectives, but also adhere to our risk tolerance as a family. It also includes an agreed upon monitoring strategy so we can effectively update the statement as our children grow and our needs change.

It is important to write this down and keep it somewhere so you can review it often. This helps remind you of the framework that you are using for decisions and helps you stay on track and not panic or choose poorly.

Diversify but don't over-diversify. Some people want to take this idea to the extreme and try to buy just a few shares of as many stocks in as many different sectors as possible, but that isn't effective. Diversification is about lowering risk, it isn't about owning as many different stocks as possible. It is more important to understand the various sectors and choose those that either complement or counterbalance each other depending on your goals. You can diversify into a few sectors and then also diversify by the choices within those sectors and that will usually be more than sufficient. It is very common for those with limited time to really learn about the sectors and various nuances of investing to employ this strategy. They think that by owning a lot of different stocks that they will insulate themselves from bad choices because they are basically picking those stocks on a whim, but the costs are much higher than you might imagine both in the short term and the long term.

Control your behavior – and that means controlling your thoughts. Having the emotional disciple not to let your feelings get the best of you is of fundamental importance. Warren Buffet said it best when he said "To invest successfully over a lifetime does not require a stratospheric IQ, unusual business insight, or inside information. What's needed is a sound intellectual framework for decisions and the ability to keep emotions from corroding that framework." I also know that most investors don't have that required emotional discipline to continually move toward their goals and are usually their own worst enemies. Wealth isn't determined by investment performance, but by investor behavior. You have the ability to invest over your lifetime and grow that wealth but it takes a great deal of emotional discipline. Otherwise, every time the market bobbles you may panic, make poor decisions and erode your future.

Account for the effects that taxes and inflation have on portfolio returns. This is an area that most people – and even some financial advisors- don't pay enough attention to. Taxes and inflation both erode your wealth over time and as you develop a long term strategy they both must be figured into the mix so you maintain realistic expectations. It is easy to look at the return on an investment and think, "Wow, I'm doing great!" But a good understanding of inflation is essential to bring that return into perspective, as you are aware that costs never go down and some years the effect of inflation makes many investments a zero sum game. Now, let's remember that there are also taxes to take into consideration. Again it's easy to not think about the fact that you will be taxed on that gain while you are excited about how well an investment is doing. Emotional Discipline is key here too because you should immediately temper that excitement with the knowledge that a percentage of that money isn't yours to keep.

When you invest in a stock, you become an owner of the business and must think and behave like a business owner. When you invest in a particular stock, think like you own the company and pay attention to how they do business. When you invest in a bond, you're become a lender to a business. Act like you're a Bank Loan Officer and watch their revenue and debt accumulation as they both determine the business' ability to repay that debt. When you think like an owner you pay attention to what is important for your investment – not the slick marketing they may do.

No one can time the market consistently over time. Good timing is something we all want. We want to buy when the stock is at a rock bottom high and then sell when it is at an all time high. Unfortunately, none of us have a crystal ball, so there is absolutely no way to know when those events will take place. The best strategy is a consistent one. You have to stay in it to win it. My own experience with day trading is a good example. I got lucky and made some good trades, but then it only took two bad ones to wipe out my entire investment account. You can't hit it out of the park on every swing and should plan for that. Some investments perform very well. Some don't and all the others fall somewhere in-between offering a modest return. Approach your investing with the understanding that market timing is another term for madness and is a losing proposition. Even today you will see or hear people who are convinced they have the perfect formula or experience to time the market but that isn't true no matter who it is. Timing the market is like chasing a ghost; about the time you think you have it, it's gone. That doesn't mean that someone can't make millions trying – they can. But they can also lose those millions very quickly, just like I lost my $82,000. Eventually, you will get caught by the law of averages and all that expertise you thought you had will be revealed as a delusion.

Volatility in market prices isn't risk and temporary decline isn't loss. There are normal ups and downs in the daily course of business, nothing more. You can think of it like turbulence on an airplane. Just because you have a little bump now and then doesn't mean the whole plane is crashing and you shouldn't panic like it is. Like Nick Murray says: "No panic, no sell. No sell, no lose". I have this quote up in my office. One of the most important functions of an excellent Investment Advisor is to help clients understand that they should not to give into fear. The decision not to sell will one day be the most important decision you ever make. However, don't assume you'll be able to make it alone because here again, those feelings of panic can overwhelm you.

At one time, I was asked by a retired ship captain to review his portfolio holdings and investment strategy. He purchased the common shares of several Canadian banks in the mid 1970s. He never sold a single share and reinvested all the dividends while he was still working. The original $370K he invested has a market value today of approximately $4.8 million which generates $78,000 per year in dividend income. He's retired now and doesn't even spend his quarterly dividend checks. He told me that as long as his dividend payments go up each year, he will keep holding his shares. He wasn't concerned about the daily price fluctuations. He was thinking and behaving like a business owner should – long term. This example taught me how important dividend growth was to total long term returns and how having emotional discipline can pay off big.

After a severe market downturn, the sky does not fall and the world does not end. People fear that their world is ending because we all fear loss much more than we hope for gain and this is a natural human tendency. Therefore, we react much more emotionally to declining markets than to rising ones. The dissatisfaction I felt when I lost my $82,000 was many times more intense than the satisfaction I felt when my $7,000 grew to $82,000. This is typical human behavior and shows exactly how our emotions can get us to make less than optimal decisions. Negative events impact us harder and we have to understand this about ourselves in order to overcome that fear and panic.

Investment information and professional investment advice are two completely different things. Information is not advice. This is something that many people have a hard time understanding. They don't realize that the market news and investment information they hear on television or read in the media (or on the internet!) is not advice. Advice is specifically tailored for your situation and your goals. Information is just that – information. It may or may not have anything to do with you or be anything that will ever help you.

One phrase that you should be especially wary of, is if you hear a news anchor ask a guest, "What does this mean for investors?" I can answer that for you right now. Nothing. It doesn't matter what it is, their information means nothing. They don't know you or what you want to accomplish so all they are spouting is rhetoric to fill air time. You hear this most often when the market takes a dip. This means nothing to investors, but yet many of the pundits and talking heads intimate that the sky is falling when it's not. Just remember, they are out to get ratings not help you with your portfolio.

In order to really understand yourself as an investor, you must understand what is really important for you. For me, it's family. The first time I traveled to Croatia was in 1979; I was 7 years old. I saw firsthand where my parents lived and got a taste for how they grew up. My mom's home was in a small village in the mountains. Her parents were farmers and their entire home was just one room, maybe 20' x 20' in size. There was no running water or electricity. I remember first thing in the morning, we would walk the donkey with a big water jug on its back to a stream four miles away. We would fill it up and head another four miles back to the house. That was our water supply for the day. The life they lived was very hard compared to what I knew yet they did what they had to do without complaint.

My parents were surrounded by unconditional love – something they passed on to me - and they always had a roof over their heads and something to eat. They were always happy as children and never knew about all the luxuries and excess in the Western World. My mom had to walk miles to school, often with no shoes and, as a child, trying to imagine that was very hard. That summer, we celebrated my brother, Mike's, 6th birthday. I remember my Grandma putting on a pot of boiling water on the wood stove while my Grandpa went out to the chicken coup to find his biggest chicken. That was the first time I ever saw a chicken run with its head cut off! This was his prized possession and the best gift he had to give us all to celebrate my brother's birthday. We had a family feast. The trip really taught me to appreciate how easy my life is and that you really don't need a lot of 'stuff' to be content.

I think back on the experience and the life I lead today. I help people reach their dreams of financial freedom and peace. Not so they can be the richest person in the cemetery, but so they can choose how they and their families live. That is what is important and it's why I do what I do - to help them accomplish those goals through well thought out financial plans and advice. While I was writing this book, I once again had the opportunity to visit Croatia and much has changed, but the people haven't. Their dreams are still there and their love of life. Its proof to me that happiness is still found in the simplest pleasures, not in piles of money.

Chapter 2

Money Matters

Chapter 2
Money Matters

Your wealth management plan affects the way you stand, the way you walk, the tone of your voice and every aspect of your daily experience. In short, your physical well-being and self-confidence are all affected by how you feel about your money. If you don't have a good plan, you feel you are always running and not getting anywhere. You must take the first job offered or opportunity that comes by. You sit nervously on life's chair since any small emergency throws your future into the hands of others. Each day is spent worrying about necessities, such as food and mortgage payments, so you can't afford to think long term. You must dart to the most immediate opportunity for ready cash. Without a plan, you will spend a life-time in a state of panic. It is a tense, frightening way to live.

On the other hand, if you have a good wealth management plan with savings and investments you can walk tall. You are able to evaluate opportunities in a relaxed way and not be rushed by economic necessity. With savings, you can afford to resign from your job and choose the lifestyle that you want for yourself and your family. A person with a plan can afford the wonderful privilege of being generous to others and think beyond themselves and the immediate needs of the day. You can take a level stare into the eyes of anyone. It shapes your personality and character.

Many people, even those with substantial income, have a hard time saving. It's important to understand that the ability to save has nothing to do with the size of your income. Many high income earners also spend everything they make and are on a tread-mill darting through life like minnows. Even though they may make millions, they are basically living paycheck to paycheck. I'd rather be living on what I earned last year instead of spending what I'll earn next year, but not everyone has learned that lesson or learned lessons as I did, so each person must come to the realization that savings are worth the perceived sacrifice. I say perceived because it's not really a sacrifice once you figure in how much more confident you will feel with money in the bank for emergencies.

Some people believe that the bigger the house the live in, the better they are doing in life. I can tell you that I've lived in a mobile home in a trailer park, a small one bedroom apartment and a 5,800 square foot home and have discovered this truth: the quality of a home has very little, in fact virtually nothing, to do with how much it costs or how big it is. Think about the houses you loved the most that you lived in throughout your life. Odds are the love you had for a particular house had zero to do with its monetary value and everything to do with how happy you were while you lived there. Think about this fact and then decide if that big home is really giving you what you want. Does it guarantee happiness or provide security for your future? No.

The same is true of the car you drive. I have a very wealthy friend who loves cars, especially sports cars. He drives a Mustang. Now, make no mistake he has millions and can drive any car he wants. So why would he choose a Mustang? He says it's as good as a BMW, a Porsche or even a Ferrari and he loves to drive it. So instead of forking over $150K +, he gets his thrills in a car that costs a fraction of that price. Also, I've never purchased a new car and never will – all vehicles are terrible investments and lose a good portion of their value the minute you drive them off the lot. In fact they are not investments at all, they are transportation and the two should not be confused! I bought a 15 month old previously owned corvette for half the price of a new one. My children now call it Daddy's "boom boom car". Still, I know many people who buy a new car each year. I find it interesting that they will purchase a $100K car each year and the day after they purchase it, the car is worth at least 10% less and they are perfectly okay with that. Yet if they purchase a stock and it lost that much the first day they would be absolutely incensed! You have to ask yourself what that purchase is giving you because it certainly isn't improving your financial position. Your emotions are once again at play and I think about that every time I see a Ferrari roaring down the street.

If you fill your life with all the best luxuries but you're too busy running around to enjoy them, you've missed the boat. There are two things to aim at in life: first to get what you want and then enjoy it. We live in a world of unlimited abundance and can get anything we want. However, only the wisest will truly enjoy what they have. Everyone else is faking it.

You may think that I'm saying that you should live in a tiny house or drive an old jalopy. Far from it; what I'm trying to get across is that you choose the things you surround yourself with and if those 'things' are not adding to your own personal happiness or to your wealth then it's time to reevaluate why you have them. You may love your Ferrari and that's great but you should own things that add to your happiness, not things just to show off to the neighbors.

Risk is Personal

When I say the word 'risk', as I will frequently in this book, I know that it means different things to different people. Almost all think that risk is bad, but really it's not. It is an evaluation tool, nothing more. In order for you to understand your financial goals and how to get there, you will have to understand how you perceive financial risk because that will give you a framework for choosing investments.

There are numerous misconceptions about financial risk but many people misperceive risk in two distinct ways. First they overestimate the risk of holding stocks over their lifetime and underestimate the risk of not holding them. In other words, they think that having an investment in stocks over the long term increases their possibility of some sort of financial disaster which is not true. Second, they think that not having stocks is somehow protecting them from financial downturns, which is also not true.

When you think about risk where money is concerned it helps to redefine the idea of money – it's not paper and coins or the number in your bank account. The real definition when we are talking about the long term is purchasing power. If you think about it from that perspective, the real risk isn't losing your money. It's outliving it.

This risk of decreased purchasing power wears many disguises and has an impact on every investment being considered. If you decide to bury your money in your garden or even leave it in a noninterest bearing cash account, you have to accept the very low probability of real capital growth, thus your purchasing power over time is a negative value due to the effects of inflation. Even a decision to do nothing has an impact on a portfolio's returns. For example, I know several investors in bonds that have been surprised to learn that their fixed income securities decline in value as interest rates increase. While this may seem obvious to some investors, we all make assumptions and think things will always go along in the same way over time just like they have so far and that is just not true with investments.

Of course there are other inherent risks associated with the stock market, real estate, and other investments. So the real task is not to try to find "risk-free" investments because they don't exist. The challenge is to decide what level of risk you are willing to assume and then to understand the implications of that choice. The recent economic recession and corresponding global financial market meltdown has led to many investors questioning their true risk tolerance and the way they perceive risk.

It amazes me that, despite their increasing sophistication, investors and advisors are still reluctant to talk about risk. But we can't talk about the rewards of investing without discussing the risks involved. They are inseparable since there is no such thing as a risk-free investment. I can't tell you how many times I've been asked the inevitable question: "John, what can I invest in over the next six months to a year that will give me a high return but has no risk?' My answer is always the same, "I don't know, but if you find out, please don't tell anyone else but me!"

To prepare yourself to invest, you must first determine your true risk tolerance. In order to do this, we need to define the word "risk". Some investors choose to define risk as the potential for loss. But I think that is a little simplistic. When I talk about risk, I like to address both the risk of fluctuation in market prices and inflation as those two forces together determine your financial outcome. It's fundamentally important to know that the fear of loss and the fluctuation in market prices are two completely separate ideas. Fear of loss is emotional, while market fluctuation is fact.

Inflation is the Enemy

I often describe inflation to my clients as a double edged sword. First, it destroys wealth by depleting accumulated capital – in short your money is worth less over time. Secondly, it reduces the purchasing power of income because everything costs more. We currently live in a historic record low interest rate environment and the current Bank of Canada published rate of inflation as I write this book is less than 2%. However, the cost to put gas in the family van, purchase groceries, heat our homes and pay our property taxes have increased by 10% or more over the last year. Stop to think about the current prices of the goods and services you consume and you may discover the same thing. Inflation sneaks up on us, and I think it will return in the coming years.

No one can say exactly when, but it is a fact that there have been inflationary cycles throughout the recorded history of mankind. You can think of inflation like an alarm clock. It sits on your night table ticking away unnoticed but at some point the alarm will sound. Your inflation alarm clock will go off with the volume cranked and you'll want to hit the snooze button but you can't stop it. What I'm really trying to say is that for most investors, inflation is an incredibly underestimated risk. For some reason they think $50K today will be $50K tomorrow and that just isn't true. A well structured investment portfolio has to account for the risk of both inflation and market volatility.

If you think back on the effect inflation has had in the past, it's easy to see how destructive it is to your purchasing power. For example, in 1950 a postage stamp in Canada was 4 cents. Today it costs 52 cents plus HST! Costs of goods and services don't decrease over time, they increase and we sometimes can forget how the cumulative power of that increase works against us. One example that I use to explain how important this is for my clients is to tell them that in 2040 (30 years), they should be prepared to pay $20 for 4 liters of milk – best case scenario. This gets their attention! That sounds outrageous, but is it? In 1980 the price of milk was between $1.20-$1.40 for 4 liters. Today it's between $4.50-$5.25, depending on where you live. That means over the last 30 years is has quadrupled. If you take today's price and quadruple it again to find the price in 2040, the price of milk will be $18-$21. No kidding.

Now reconsider how much money you thought you might need to retire. Did it account for paying $20 for a gallon of milk? That's what I mean when I say that inflation is widely underestimated by both investors and their financial advisors. When you are estimating what you might need to live your current lifestyle, if those estimations are based on faulty assumptions that don't adequately account for things like inflation, your goals will fall very short and that will affect how you live the remainder of your life so it's no small thing.

Fear is Debilitating

What you fear the most in life, owns you, controls you, and limits you. As a child, I used to struggle with the fear of heights, but I fought it. Years later, I jumped out of plane at 13,000 feet to go sky diving and I was fine. I was better than fine, in fact, I was great! I can't wait to do it again. If I could have one foolish child-like wish come true it would be to have the ability to fly like a bird. So, on my bucket list is to fly a personal jet pack!

Now just imagine if I hadn't tackled that fear head on. I would have avoided anything that I perceived to be precarious, like hiking in the mountains or even enjoying the beautiful view from the top of a skyscraper and I certainly would have never felt the thrill of jumping out of an airplane. I also might have transferred that fear to my children and that would have been sad – yet many people transfer their fears about money to their kids and this inhibits their own ability to succeed. Overcoming fear is freedom; giving into fear is incarceration. As we age, more and more of those things we fear center around money and our financial wellbeing.

Fear cripples many and prevents them from making good decisions. It limits the ability to enjoy even the simplest things in life and in some cases stops people from achieving financial independence. I have clients who refuse to invest in anything other than guaranteed investment certificates(GICs) and they rely on the interest income to supplement their retirement income. Given that interest rates are currently at historic lows, the after tax and inflation adjusted return on these investments is negative. For example, a one year GIC pays 1.75%.

In Ontario, the highest marginal tax rate is 46% bringing the after-tax return to 0.95%. With the current inflation rate in Canada at 2.1%, the return on investment is -1.15%! So, you're guaranteed to lose money today investing in a GIC. However, some clients when I suggest that they can earn a tax efficient dividend yield of 4% that keeps growing by owning the highest quality Canadian bank and utility common shares, they look like I'm suggesting they jump out of an airplane! They don't fear the investment itself, what they really fear is reading the fluctuating market values on their monthly statements. It is this fear that cripples them from actually making money and so their holdings are diminished more and more as time goes by.

We are the masters and money is the servant. It's never the other way around. People with financial fears think that money is the master. I've seen many people so fearful that they won't spend a dime or enjoy anything they have earned and this is nothing more than fear rearing its head. If you are able to release that fear and invest wisely, then money flows back to you allowing you the freedom to really live and not worry that you will outlive your resources.

Warren Buffett is widely considered to be one of the greatest investors of all time, but if you were to ask him who he thinks is the greatest investor he would probably mention one man, his teacher, Benjamin Graham who taught Warren to always invest with a margin of safety. Margin of safety is the principle of buying a security at a significant discount to its intrinsic value, which is thought to not only provide high-return opportunities, but also to minimize the downside risk of an investment. It's like getting something on sale. The asset is still just as valuable as the retail price, but it's currently priced less. In simple terms, Graham's goal was to buy assets worth $1 for $0.50. To Graham, these business assets may have been valuable because of their stable earning power or simply because of their liquid cash value. It wasn't uncommon, for example, for Graham to invest in stocks where the liquid assets on the balance sheet (net of all debt) were worth more than the total market capital of the company.

The second thing Warren Buffet learned from his teacher was to expect volatility and profit from it rather than fear it. Investing in stocks means dealing with volatility. Instead of running for the exit during times of market stress, the smart investor greets downturns as chances to find great investments. Graham illustrated this with the analogy of "Mr. Market", the imaginary business partner of each and every investor.

Mr. Market offers investors a daily price quote at which he would either buy an investor out or sell his share of the business. Sometimes, he will be excited about the prospects for the business and quote a high price. At other times, he is depressed about the business's prospects and will quote a low price.

Because the stock market has these same emotions, the lesson here is that you shouldn't let Mr. Market's views dictate your own emotions, or worse, lead you in your investment decisions. Instead, you should form your own estimates of the business value based on a sound and rational examination of the facts.

Furthermore, you should only buy when the price offered makes sense and sell when the price becomes too high. Put another way, the market will fluctuate - sometimes wildly - but rather than fearing volatility, use it to your advantage to get bargains in the market or to sell out when your holdings become way overvalued.

There is no question that the markets challenge your emotions. What's difficult about investing isn't getting the right facts. What's difficult is learning how to put them to work. This is perhaps the biggest weakness of individual investors in that they can't get past the emotional aspect to put the facts to work. Now, make no mistake that will say they are unemotional and they think they can handle volatility, but the second the market goes into the red they are the first to call me. Step back from the situation and think about how you invest. Are you really unemotional? The answer is probably no.

There are also two big secrets that most investors aren't aware of. The first of these is that, on the whole, individual stock selection doesn't really matter. I hear that sucking sound you're making right now, but you read that right. Individual stock selections aren't the end all, be all. What really matters, over the long term, is asset allocation decisions which is all about when you buy. It's not what specific stocks you buy. It's the decision of when you buy stocks versus when you buy bonds, gold, cash, real estate, or other investments that really matters.

Several academic studies demonstrate why portfolio asset allocation is far more important in determining your results than simply which stocks or bonds you buy. The first (Brinson) was published in 1986. And Ibbotson and Kaplan published the best study (in my opinion) in 2000. The latter looked at 94 U.S. mutual funds and several asset classes. The researchers concluded the differences in asset allocation among the funds explained virtually 100% of the variance in their returns. Differences in stock picks made virtually no difference whatsoever to total portfolio returns. The takeaway from these studies is simple: asset allocation is far more important to your total portfolio return than stock picking. That's why most professional investors (like the top hedge-fund managers) allow analysts to do the stock picking, while they focus almost exclusively on the core allocation decisions.

On the other hand, most individual investors don't spend any time or effort on managing asset allocation. They're typically fully invested in stocks all the time. Most individual investors don't even know how to buy bonds (which is a critical component of asset allocation), and they do a terrible job at position sizing, another critical component. The size of the position goes back to the amount of risk involved and getting this one component wrong can put way too much capital at risk. Remember when I lost my $82,000 on two trades? This was a huge error in position sizing. I had two large positions which put my money at a much greater risk than if I'd had many small positions.

The second secret is how to properly value a security. In my experience, most individual investors have zero ability to calculate even the most basic measures of value in either a stock or a bond. How can you buy a stock or a bond without knowing how to value it? And yet, that is what most individual investors do every single time they buy a stock. They are basically guessing or listening to someone else's guessing.

Believe it or not, most people probably believe a $20 stock is twice as valuable as a $10 stock. It is nearly impossible to explain to them that the price of a stock has nothing to do with its value. With study, the fair value of a stock can be determined. However, rather than study the financial statements and outlook for sales and/or profit growth, most individual investors prefer to focus on changes in price as determiner of value. By doing so, they behave like short term traders instead of long term business owners. This is how many investors get into trouble and lose money, sometimes big money.

If you master and use both these secrets together (asset allocation and proper valuation), you can become a vastly improved investor and your portfolio will show the gains to prove it.

The Real Problem

Pogo, a famous philosopher, once said "We have met the enemy...and he is us!" Much of the grief investors experience is self-inflicted. Their feelings, attitudes, desires, beliefs and biases they have accumulated from both good and bad experiences prohibit them from having a life time of investment success. Investors want to behave rationally but can't do it because we are all emotional beings. One of the more dangerous types of investors is the one who believes they are 100% rational at all times. They aren't and by telling themselves this lie they can't see how much damage they are really doing to their own portfolio. None of us are immune to the effect fear can have nor are we able to completely deny those emotions. What we can do is learn not to make fear driven decisions. Wealth is not determined by investment performance but by investor behavior so it is that behavior we must focus on to improve our investing strategies.

Think about the way the market fluctuates when new reports come out that show the unemployment rate or the economic outlook. The market reacts and stock prices fluctuate. Does that mean the value of the company you are invested in suddenly fluctuates? No, the value is pretty much the same as it was the day before, barring any earthshaking revelations from the company. Most people don't get this. All they see is the price drop; they don't realize it's a result of investor behavior, not a real time determination of value.

Remember that people fear loss much more than they hope for gain. Therefore, they react much more emotionally to declining markets than rising markets – and investors are people just like you. Learning to objectively view market fluctuations, and understand the real value to be had, is a key step to becoming the type of investor that wins over the long run and isn't worried by the short term fluctuations.

Years ago, I had the privilege of working with Ted Parsons. Ted is a retired executive of a global insurance company. He helped me develop and implement several business succession plans and estate plans for some of my ultra high net worth clients. Ted's expertise and experience is second to none. He taught me how to really understand what's going on in a person's heart and mind by making an emotional connection to their fears, dreams and desires. He has become a good friend and ongoing mentor over the years. Having spent forty years in the Financial Service business, Ted has always been amazed at how many business and professional people fail to prepare adequately for their future. Here is an example he used to share with me:

In 1923, a group of the world's most successful financiers met at the Edgewater Hotel in Chicago.

Present were:

- The president of the largest steel company in the USA
- The president of the largest utility company in the USA
- The greatest wheat speculator in the world
- The president of the New York Stock Exchange
- A member of the US President's Cabinet
- The greatest "bear" in Wall Street
- The president of the Bank of International Settlements
- The head of the world's greatest monopoly

Collectively, these tycoons controlled more wealth then there was in the United States Treasury at the time. For years newspapers and magazines had been printing their success stories and urging the youth of the nation to follow their example.

Twenty five years later, let's see what happened to these men:

- The president of the steel company – Charles Schwab – lived on borrowed money the last five years of his life, and died broke.
- The president of the largest utility company – Samuel Insull – died flat broke.
- The wheat speculator – Arthur Cutter – died abroad, insolvent.
- The president of the New York Stock Exchange – Richard Whitney – was incarcerated then eventually released from Sing Sing federal penitentiary.
- The President's Cabinet Member – Albert Fall – was pardoned from prison, so he could die at home.
- The Wall Street "bear" – Jesse Livermore – committed suicide.
- The president of the Bank of International Settlements – Leon Fraser – committed suicide.
- The monopoly head – Ivar Krueger – committed suicide.

All of these men had learned how to make money, but not one of them had learned to prepare for his future. Ultimately, all of the wealth they accumulated over their lifetimes disappeared and led to many a tragic end.

I believe that many of our world's financial problems are a result of financial ignorance. That's why we've made financial education our #1 priority. I believe a financially intelligent people will be a prosperous people and that lives can be transformed through financial education. That's why I've made financial education for my children a priority.

I'm a big fan of Robert Kiosk, the author of Rich Dad Poor Dad which is the best selling personal finance book of all time. The philosophy of Rich Dad was built from a simple lesson learned by Robert Kiyosaki at an early age. He had two dads—one rich and one poor.

Robert's poor dad, his natural father, was highly educated, the head of the Hawaiian school system, and enjoyed a decent salary. Yet, he constantly complained about having no money and continually said, "I can't afford it."

Robert's rich dad, his best friend's father, was a dropout, was building a business, and didn't have much money. Yet, he constantly enjoyed the finer things in life and always asked, "How can I afford it?"

The contrast between Robert's two dads taught him a great lesson. Robert realized his poor dad's outlook suppressed his dreams and closed his mind to the possibility of financial freedom. He died penniless and full of regret. His rich dad's outlook elevated his dreams and opened his mind to life's possibilities. He achieved great wealth, financial freedom, and enjoyed life to the fullest.

Robert wasn't content with retirement, however, and fueled by the passion to teach the financial wisdom of his rich dad, Robert created his financial board game, CASH FLOW FOR KIDS. This fun, fast-paced educational board game teaches basic concepts of accounting, finance, and investing by giving children the opportunity to learn and apply real-life decisions with real-life consequences.

This financial board game has become a favorite in our home. It's truly wonderful to help my children grow their financial IQ at a young age. I grin from ear to ear when one of my children asks if we can all play this board game together!

This past summer, my 6 year old son Johnny started a lawn care business! He knocked on neighbors doors and asked if he could pull the weeds and cut the grass. After landing his first deal, he recruited two of his friends to work for him. I have seen them load their work wagon with all the lawn care equipment that they could find at home. They worked on one front yard all afternoon. When we called Johnny in for supper, he came running home and couldn't wait to tell us about his first day in business. He earned $15 and had a happy customer who referred him to his neighbor!

By putting their financial knowledge in action, my children have gained valuable experience and confidence that will translate into them understanding the rules of the rich.

You also have the opportunity to prepare and plan your way to a great future no matter your age or circumstance. You can start at any time and I encourage you not to wait; there is never a better time than right now.

Chapter 3

The Right Fit

Chapter 3
The Right Fit

If you want to have the kind of financial plan that meets your goals over the long term then it is essential that you find a financial professional that knows and understands your goals and has your best interests at heart. Of course finding the right person is one of the biggest concerns investors have. The relationship is key to your long term success and financial well being and cannot be taken lightly. You should evaluate several advisors before making your selection and to help you in that endeavor, I've come up with a list of qualities to look for in a good financial manager as well as a list of questions to ask to help expose any weak areas or potential problems.

Trust, mutual respect, empathy and a shared sense of purpose should be the hallmarks of your relationship with your lifetime wealth manager. Then comes competence and that can be harder to gauge. It has been my experience that people don't care what you know until they know and feel that you really care about them. The advisor who's really right for you listens to you and cares about you. You need to feel the advisor's genuine interest in you because his desire to do good for you and your family is of paramount importance. When you sit down with an advisor you will immediately feel a connection with them as a person – or not. If you don't then you have to ask yourself why. Often when we are in an unfamiliar situation we push aside or ignore those initial impressions but they are the very instincts that we need to listen to. Even someone that has no real competence can present an argument that might win you over, but you can still feel if there is a disconnect with that individual as a person and at that point, you should step back and reconsider.

I was once a young money manager and while there is nothing wrong with being young, I also know that experience is invaluable. You want a money manager that has personally been through several economic cycles. They will have that personal experience of investor panic and recovery as well as knowing what rookie mistakes not to make. You also want to know that they will be around a year from now. A large percentage of the young people who start out in this business quit or move on within their first three years. A wealth plan is a long term lifelong plan and you want someone who really has a heart for helping you meet your goals and who loves the business.

Once a wealth management plan is in place, a critical function of your wealth manager will be to help you manage your emotions and not to give in to panic and fear in times of financial crisis. The decision not to panic and sell is the most important investment decision you ever make but don't assume you'll be able to make this decision alone due to the impact of emotions that we already discussed. You have to rely on the relationship with your wealth manager and lean on them when your emotions may be running high. That means you must trust and respect the opinion of the wealth manager you choose and if you know that will be hard due to the advisors age (or any other reason) then you need to choose someone else. If you put a plan in place, but don't respect the person who crafted it than you can easily make bad decisions in a time of crisis as you won't listen to what they have to say. As you evaluate the person you are considering to manage your plan, ask yourself, "Can I trust this person to tell me the hard truths and if they do, will I accept their advice and professional judgment or just get angry and do it my way?" It's important to make that decision before you are in crisis and think about how you will respond when they call and tell you something you may not want to hear. Will you be grateful that they are looking out for your best interest or will you most likely respond poorly?

It almost goes without saying that you choose someone properly licensed and able to professionally manage money. But I still mention it here because I'm amazed at the number of high net worth people who listen to advice from their fishing buddies all the way to their brother in law– none of whom have any idea what they are talking about – and then make investment decisions based on hearsay. There are stringent regulatory requirements for financial advisors and money managers and that gives you a certain level of security that your money is being handled with the utmost fiduciary responsibility.

As you interview advisors, don't be afraid to get personal with them. It is very important that you share similar beliefs about money and wealth. This is vital because you will be communicating about things that affect your life for the long term and you don't want miscommunication that stems from differing beliefs about what is important. Unfortunately, you frequently see financial advisors who dispense advice all day long about how to manage your wealth, but take none of that advice for themselves. I've even known stock brokers that own no stocks, insurance agents that carry little to no insurance and estate planners who have no will! Are those really the people you want taking care of your money?

The Advisor Types

There are some standard personality types that you may encounter as you go about searching for your own personal wealth manager. Some are humorous and others more serious, but it's important that you be able to recognize these types and understand what hiring them might mean for your portfolio over the long term.

The Cowboy - Many young or inexperienced advisors fall into this category – I was even one of them way back when I managed my $82,000 into the ground!. They are always swinging for the fences, going for that grand slam, the big score. They tend to operate on the belief that to triumph without risk is to win without glory. Therefore, they may risk much more than you are comfortable with in order to impress you with a big score. The cowboy investment advisor speculates on new start-up and/or mining ventures with a very low probability of a favorable outcome. They are excited and see only the upside potential with little or no consideration on the downside risks. They are 'best case scenario' focused and rarely give the possibility for a poor outcome adequate weight. I have a drawer in one of my filing cabinets filled with worthless stock certificates I've collected over the years from clients who bring them into my office to inquire about an investment they made years ago with their stock broker who's now moved on or who has disappeared. I could wallpaper my office with them as they were made by someone seeking a big score, not one seeking to help their client over the long haul so they are worthless. Now I'm not saying that you can never make a somewhat speculative investment, I'm just cautioning you that it be done with full disclosure and perhaps using a very small percentage of your capital while the remaining portion is invested in a more prudent manner. It is fun to hit a big score on occasion, but that small thrill in no way will make up for a big loss which is more than likely with a highly speculative investment.

Milton the Miser – This type of financial advisor is all about protection, not growth, to the point that they will not risk anything. While at first glance you may think this is a good thing, remember back to our discussion about inflation. If you are only investing in cash or GICs or other investments that are considered completely 'safe' you are not moving forward. In fact, you are not even treading water! You are actually allowing inflation to rob you of your capital over time. So rather than helping you, this type of advisor is allowing your portfolio to decrease each and every year. By trying to play it safe, this advisor fails to structure the portfolio to be protected from the ongoing ravages of inflation and is more concerned with ensuring little or no volatility appears on the client's monthly statements. The reason most people don't like volatility is that it feeds right back into their fear that they will lose money. Yet without planning for inflation they are already leaking capital with no end in sight. I've seen this occur with advisors that are either scared of the market themselves, or scared of their clients becoming angry. Either way they are not concerned with the client's long term financial wellbeing and that spells disaster for the client.

The Oracle – This type of advisor believes in Warren Buffett's principles of investing. After careful study, one should act like a business owner and invest only in businesses (not "stocks") that he understands with a margin of safety, a sustainable competitive advantage (an economic moat), and predictable future earnings. The Oracle welcomes volatility and is able to capitalize on opportunities when others are fearful. His favorite holding period is forever. This type of advisor has a basic core understanding of the principles of successful investing. You'd be amazed at the financial advisors who have no grasp of these concepts. Investing is about growing business, not trading or buying stocks and having an advisor that is well grounded in this knowledge is one of the most important attributes your future wealth manager can exhibit.

Pension Pete (The Pension Fund Manager) – This advisor's investment philosophy is based on growing capital for clients in a low risk manner and is founded upon conservative, time proven principles of fundamental investing. High quality diversified portfolios are constructed and managed that are designed to preserve the real purchasing power of its clients' funds with minimal risk to achieve long-term growth. This investment approach has produced consistent returns through changing economic environments for years and has been proven effective. This approach has been particularly effective in minimizing the volatility prevalent in today's global markets and so investors can have faith that this type of plan will survive the various twists and turns of the broader global markets. This advisor follows a low risk approach toward the management of both equities and fixed income investments. There is no speculation. They invest in proven, well-managed, high quality companies which are financially sound which serves to minimize portfolio risk. This approach is reinforced through extensive security analysis and ongoing research. The advisor doesn't just sit back and let it ride. He is constantly reevaluating and updating each position and company analysis. He believes high quality equities are the best source of long-term growth for a portfolio, while bonds should provide income to meet current requirements. Risk controls are used to reduce volatility in the short term and preserve capital over the long term.

There are many different types of investors and most are some type of mix of these personalities but I would tell you that the best mix is part Oracle and part Pension Pete. This mix gives you a wealth manager who understands the reality of market evaluation and is able to create a mix that will serve your long term needs while lowering excessive amounts of risk. They don't take the approach of no risk, but they vastly limit the effect that risk has on portfolio performance.

The Interview

When you set an appointment to meet with an advisor, there are several questions that you should ask. The responses (or lack thereof) will help you gauge not only the openness and honesty of the advisor, but will give you some insight to their business and how they work.

Tough Questions to Ask a Potential Wealth Manager

1. How many clients have you lost and why did they leave?

I have been asked this before and it is a fair question. I choose to answer openly and talk about the few situations where this has occurred and the circumstances. My intention is to demonstrate that I'm not perfect and I have nothing to hide. I believe this is of fundamental importance to establishing trust in an advisory relationship.

Asking such a direct question about an advisor's business will make them uncomfortable and that is good. You will be able to tell if the person is ashamed or if they gloss over it wanting to move on.

Both are indications that they will act in a similar fashion if something goes wrong with your financial plan. You want a person who will take responsibility for their actions and explain situations fully, no matter what.

2. What is your typical client's profile?

This is a question that I wish all prospective clients referred to me would ask in our initial consultation. I can't be all things to all people. But I am exceptional at providing wealth management planning, advice and service to professionals, small business owners and retirees with net a net worth in excess of $2 million. The answer to this question will help you decide if the wealth advisor is a good fit for you or not. Some specialize in corporate executives, others in young families that are just getting started, while others may specialize in certain professional groups such as doctors or lawyers. Each of these groups of people has different goals and needs and you really want someone who is very familiar with the group that you fall into. Just because someone handles large amounts of money doesn't mean they will really understand your situation so go with someone who has extensive experience with clients very similar to you.

3. Do you provide a written financial plan and an investment policy statement? If so, how often is it reviewed?

In order for your wealth advisor to really understand your current financial situation and objectives, it must be documented. This roadmap clearly outlines where you are now and where you want to go. Furthermore, it is a blueprint to measure progress against and account for changes in your life along the way. If your wealth advisor isn't providing you with a written financial plan, ask why. Do they not want documentation that their performance will be gauged against?

Perhaps they don't want the extra paperwork and insist that you 'trust' them. This is your long term financial life that you are dealing with so the idea of trusting someone blindly should never be a consideration. Yes you want someone very trustworthy, but you also want to verify the plan they have in mind and compare results along the way as things change. You also want to be sure you have regular face to face access to that person if need be. There is nothing more frustrating than developing a plan, but then never being able to check up on that plan or get in touch with your advisor. Good customer service and communication is vital to an ongoing relationship.

4. How do you get paid?

This is an awkward question for many people to ask, but it is important that you understand how they are compensated in order to figure out what type of advisor is best for you over the long term. Remember you are interviewing them for the job, they are not interviewing you to take you on as a client so don't be shy about asking. In the money management business there are four main compensation models.

These are Salary, Salary + Bonus, Commission-based, and Fee-based. Each model has its advantages and disadvantages, depending on both the size of your portfolio, the type of investor you are and your other wealth management needs.

Before you can determine which type of financial advisor is best for you, it helps to get a basic idea of the different compensation options they could work under. It's important to know, but the type of compensation method used shouldn't be the sole decision making criteria when choosing an advisor.

There's much more to it than just that. You might think from a dollars and cents perspective that one option is clearly better than the other, but in many cases I would argue it is not that cut and dry. Also, these differences don't necessarily speak to the actual abilities or individual attributes of the financial advisor, it is just one factor to consider.

Salary Only

There are a handful of financial advisors in Canada that are paid by salary only. They do not receive bonuses or commissions on top of a base salary.

Pros:
- Advisor has no conflict of interest to put you into any one product
- May have low investment minimums

Cons:
- Advisor has no incentive to go above and beyond to exceed your expectations because they continue to earn their salary as long as they perform basic functions

- Turnover can be high as advisors may leave for a higher paying model after establishing relationships with clients (may try to take them to their new employer), or just gain experience and desire to grow, face new challenges
- Limited product and service offering.

Salary plus Bonus

This is the normal structure you will find at the bank branch level. These in-house financial advisors will be paid a base salary and can earn a bonus that can double their base salary based on what products they sell to clients. They may get rewarded for bringing in business to other areas of the bank such as the mortgage department, small business banking, referring up to the full service brokerage or commercial banking.

Pros:

- One stop shopping for all of your basic financial needs can be handled at your local bank branch
- Brand name of a big regulated institution is comforting to many people
- Advisor doesn't have to spend a lot of time prospecting as branch already has clients doing business with them
- No investment minimums and will readily talk to new/small investors

Cons:

- Bonus structure puts emphasis on products
- Advisor may deal with 1,000+ clients – makes it harder to develop deep advisor-client relationship
- Investment solutions are limited with emphasis on proprietary portfolios
- Less competitive on costs as portfolios grow in size

Commission-Based

There are a number of different commission based advisors out there. On the investing side, some only offer mutual funds and GICs, others offer those as well as stocks and bonds and securities (such as hedge funds or options), while still others also offer segregated funds issued by insurance companies.

Pros:
- Advisor is rewarded for actively finding and identifying solutions for the client's wealth management needs.
- Advisor can be rewarded when recommendations work (income goes up when your portfolio grows and income decreases when your portfolio decreases).
- Access to a broad wealth management product and service offering.

Cons:
- Advisor has conflict of interest: can be focused more on product, may recommend investing over debt reduction due to compensation difference (for example)
- Fees embedded in products make it hard to determine what you're paying for products and advice
- Advisor may be more motivated to start relationship and less motivated to maintain relationship
- Advisors can be urged to use higher risk products not necessarily in their clients best interest (as higher risk products can pay higher commissions)

Fee-Based

Fees that are earned by fee-based advisors are usually know as Client Advisory Fees and are based on a flat percentage of the overall household portfolio size as opposed to being more transactional.

Pros:
- Fees are transparent and detailed on all statements, making it easier to see what you are paying for advice.
- Fees are all inclusive for all ongoing wealth management planning, advice and service.
- Advisor is rewarded when investment strategy works (income increases when your portfolio grows, income decreases when your portfolio shrinks). Therefore, interests are aligned.
- Fees may be tax deductible as investment carrying costs for non-registered accounts.
- Fees may be tiered, meaning they are reduced as your portfolio grows.

- Asset class pricing allows for different fee structures for different asset classes. For example, fee structure for fixed income is lower than for equities or option.
- Access to unlimited product and service offering from multiple providers.

Cons:

- Advisor may have a high minimum portfolio size requirement, almost always in the 6-figure range
- Some advisors only offer investment management and others offer financial planning on top of investment management – you need to make sure you are comparing apples to apples. Investment management and financial planning at 1.25% might be better than just investment management at 1.00% (for example)
- Some fee-based advisors charge an advisory fee in addition to any related product fee (MER on a mutual fund or ETF for example). By doing so, they're double dipping.
- Advisor can be very selective on which clients they choose to serve.

I've been a fee-based wealth advisor for the last 14 years. I believe that compensation drives motivation and a fee-based advisory relationship is in my client's best interests. If they make money, I make money. Fees are fully transparent and known up front in writing. Therefore, the stage is set for building a foundation for a long term advisory relationship based on mutual trust. They have no worry that there is a hidden financial motivation behind the advice I'm giving or product I'm suggesting.

If you're considering a fee-based wealth advisor, I see the main question as this: will working with a fee-based advisor add more than 1% (or whatever the percentage cost they are charging) to your total life return? Does it seem reasonable to you that your wealth advisor's counsel will:

a) Increase your return by more than the percentage cost per year,
b) save you more than the percentage cost in one year in mistakes you were advised not to make

c) save you time, effort and provide you with financial piece of mind that is worth more than the percentage cost per year to you

OR

d) All of the above?

Finally, a portion of my advisory fees each year are paid to me by my firm in the form of deferred share units. This form of deferred compensation is designed to retain and reward the wealth advisor for providing an exceptional client experience for the very long term. In doing so, I'm motivated and focused on building and maintaining client advisory relationships for the next 30 years. I'm not going away. This is part of the reason that I take a multi-generational family approach to wealth management. My objective is to provide my client's with solutions to all of their wealth accumulation, preservation and transition needs. In order to do this and be 100% committed, my compensation model is aligned with this long term client advisory approach.

No matter which model you feel works best for you at this stage of your life, the important thing is to understand the options and make an informed choice that will work for you over the long term and give you the advice and security that your portfolio deserves.

Chapter 4

You Are HERE

Chapter 4
You Are HERE

As we all navigate our daily lives, we don't often give a lot of thought (or any) to our long term financial plan. In fact, many people have no plan – and even worse, they have no plan to have a plan! If you don't have clear, concise goals that you are working toward, how will you ever achieve the life you want? How will you even know where you stand right now?

I speak with people every day who have no overall financial goals. They have a vague idea of the kind of life they would like to lead over the next few decades but everything is very general and certainly not written down in a way that will help them get there. One of the most interesting things that occurs is when I ask a client where they think they stand financially.

Most people, especially those with a high net worth, will tell you that they know exactly where they stand, or that they have a pretty good idea. But when I get through analyzing all the data and financial statements they bring me, it is shocking to see how far off they are. Some really do have a good idea but those people are few and far between, and most of the rest are not near as well off as they thought given what they say they would like to accomplish financially.

I've given a great deal of thought to the reasons behind this disparity and I know for a fact that it's not math. We can all add up how much we have in assets and how much we own in obligations and then easily figure a rough net worth. But we don't actually sit down and do it very often (if ever). Why? I believe the answer lies in our emotional ties to what money means and says about us as individuals. We believe the best and discount the negative so in our minds we are more stable than we appear. It is like that person who lives paycheck to paycheck just merrily skipping along through life assuming everything is great, and it is until one small unexpected event occurs and suddenly they are overwhelmed because they have no safety net. They have not considered the extensive cost of being cash poor with few options. Wealthy people get themselves into this exact same position. They underestimate how costly it can be to have their wealth in hard assets so when their cash flow takes a hit they are suddenly broke.

We also don't consider how expensive the future will be. We like to think that things will go on as they always have and our perception is that they do, but it is not reality. Costs and obligations creep up on us and as our cash flow rises, we often increase our standard of living to match, therefore absorbing the extra cash that should be going to pay for our future. My wife and I are no exception. There are certain things that we believe are priorities for our family and we have to plan for them just like anyone else and a good example is the plan we made for our children's college education.

The average 4 year undergraduate degree in Canada in 2009 cost just over $53,000 for a student living at home and more than $80,000 for a student who lived away from home. (TD Economics report, May 17, 2010: "Post-Secondary Education is a Smart Route to a Brighter Future for Canadians".)

That's a lot of money; but as a parent, you would probably like your child to obtain a post-secondary education, and the brighter prospects that go with it. The good news is you have time on your side to help make it possible. If you start saving now — even a modest amount each month — it will really make a difference to your child's future.

My daughter Anna is now 4. She has 14 years to go before she attends college or university starting in 2025. Based on a 5% annual rate of increase in tuition and related post secondary education costs, Anna will need $170,675 to finance an undergraduate degree away from home! Anna's Registered Education Savings Plan (RESP) currently has $28,000. To reach our education savings goal for Anna of $170,675, we're saving $393.06/month inside her RESP.

The table below shows accumulation and depletion of savings required to finance Anna's 4 year undergraduate degree by investing in a RESP.

Year	Monthly Savings for Anna	Total Monthly Savings for Grant	Total Monthly Savings	Market Value RESP Savings	Annual Education Costs
2011	$393.06	$33.33	$426.39	$34,653.25	$0.00
2012	$393.06	$33.33	$426.39	$41,639.16	$0.00
2013	$393.06	$33.33	$426.39	$48,974.36	$0.00
2014	$393.06	$33.33	$426.39	$56,676.32	$0.00
2015	$393.06	$33.33	$426.39	$64,763.39	$0.00
2016	$393.06	$33.33	$426.39	$73,254.80	$0.00
2017	$393.06	$33.33	$426.39	$82,170.79	$0.00
2018	$393.06	$33.33	$426.39	$91,532.57	$0.00
2019	$393.06	$33.33	$426.39	$101,362.45	$0.00
2020	$393.06	$33.33	$426.39	$111,683.82	$0.00
2021	$393.06	$33.33	$426.39	$122,521.26	$0.00
2022	$393.06	$33.33	$426.39	$133,900.57	$0.00
2023	$393.06	$33.33	$426.39	$145,848.84	$0.00
2024	$393.06	$33.33	$426.39	$158,394.53	$0.00
2025	$0.00	$0.00	$0.00	$124,735.69	$39,598.63
2026	$0.00	$0.00	$0.00	$87,314.98	$41,578.56
2027	$0.00	$0.00	$0.00	$45,840.37	$43,657.49
2028	$0.00	$0.00	$0.00	$0.00	$45,840.37

The interesting thing about life is that when the budget is strained, there is never just one problem that hits us. Suddenly a child's tuition jumps 10%, the air conditioning unit in the house dies, and we may have an accident that keeps us from earning as we normally would. The compounding effect of these types of changes can devastate our financial well-being even if we think we have a sufficient emergency fund. While this is not really meant to scare you, unfortunately we often don't see the necessity of planning until we are scared so it is helpful to consider the what ifs and make a plan before we are forced to.

One of the things I've found is there's a lot of confusion today about money and the idea of wealth. We're often told as children that the best things in life are free. That money doesn't buy love, friendship, or happiness and that those ingredients are necessary to live a truly wealthy life. Of course, those things are technically true. But it's not the whole truth. Money gives you choices. Money represents freedom. No one is truly free who is a slave to his job, his creditors, or his circumstances yet even people with extremely high volumes of cash flow often don't feel wealthy. I recently watched a candid interview with Oprah Winfrey as she was being asked why she was leaving her talk show after 25 years.

Of course Oprah is one of the wealthiest people on earth and has the freedom to do anything she wants. When asked why she was stopping her show, she cited her quality of life and the fact that she can't keep raising the bar forever as she can't keep up physically or emotionally. I believe that many entrepreneurs and corporate executives get to this point in their careers. They realize that they have actually attained the idea of 'wealth' as far as how much money they have in the bank, but they are missing out on the full definition of wealth because their lives are unbalanced. They have traded some of those 'free' and wonderful things in life to succeed and once they achieve those dreams, they aren't as happy as they want to be or aren't living a fulfilled life. They want to step back from all the work and gain some balance, but they can't do that if they don't have a solid financial plan to help them.

I think everyone has a right, if not an obligation, to pursue some kind of financial independence, whether that means becoming quite wealthy or just getting out from under your credit card debt. But beyond that, it's clear there are things much more important than money.

I think everyone stops and thinks from time to time, "Am I really pursuing a good life? Am I going to look back one day and say that I lived a meaningful life?" No one wants to feel like they've spent their days fully engaged in something that really didn't matter or prevented them from true achieving happiness – yet we still must earn money.

At the same time, these ideas are so personal and sensitive that most people rarely talk about them. You could know someone for decades and never really know their inner-most beliefs about wealth, except to the extent that you could extrapolate them from their behavior. As a financial advisor, I frequently meet people who truly feel that talk about inner beliefs and happiness has no place in creating a financial plan, but they are wrong. The two are interdependent because you can't pursue one without understanding the other! When a client tells me to just make a plan and skip the introspection, then I know we have a problem. You can't slap a plan on your finances like a bandage and think it will help you meet your goals. The real issues still fester and ooze under the surface and will always get in the way unless dealt with directly.

We all go through school and learn about various subjects that we rarely use in our day-to-day lives, but we're taught very little – if anything – about the best ways to live, how to achieve financial prosperity, or what happiness is let alone how to get there. You're pretty much on your own as far as figuring out how to create a prosperous, happy life. So I think for many people there's a desire to explore these issues in more depth, whether they realize it or not and because money and finances are such emotionally charged subjects, these issues are brought to the surface.

One concept that I talk to my clients about in detail is the perspective we each carry with us about money and wealth and what effect this can have. We are each a product of different experiences and influences so every person's perspective will be slightly different. There's an old story about a man who's walking along and sees these workers carrying heavy stones in wheelbarrows. He stops the first one and says, "Do you mind if I ask what you're doing?" The guy looks up and replies, "What does it look like I'm doing? I'm hauling rocks," and he keeps going.

The man stops the next guy and he says, "Do you mind if I ask what you're doing?" And that guy replies, "We're putting up a wall," and he keeps going.

The man's curiosity is still not satisfied, so he stops a third fellow and says, "I'm sorry, but could you tell me what you are doing?" That guys stops, puts his wheelbarrow down, wipes his brow, and replies, "We're building a cathedral."

Now all three workers are doing the exact same thing, but look at the different perspectives they have of what they are accomplishing. They could be thinking they're just hauling rocks, or they could be thinking they're doing something great, something meaningful.

We all go through life this way and our unique perspective colors what we experience. For example, let's say you have three people, each with a net worth of ten million dollars. One man may feel he is infinitely wealthy and that he has achieved a great and mighty existence. He lives life with joy and revels in the experience of sharing his good fortune with family and friends so he pays attention to investing wisely – always looking to, and planning for, the future.

The second person may feel that she is doing well, but still must work hard to add to that balance and only when she has 20 million will she have the freedom to do what makes her happy. She doesn't really enjoy a lot outside work because she doesn't feel she's 'earned' it yet so she is constantly stuck in the present and doesn't pay a lot of attention to her investments. The third person may fear losing that money and the security he has built over a lifetime. He thinks about all the years it took to build that financial fort and now is in 'protect' mode. He refuses to invest in anything but the safest investments and in doing so is actually tearing down his fort brick by brick. He is stuck in the past.

Each of these people have the same financial situation, but they all have differing perspectives of what that money meant and thus lived very different lives. You choose the kind of life you live, but you also choose your perspective. As you think about your own financial situation, you must become aware of the perspective you are viewing it from in order to know if your emotions are getting in the way of living the life you want and making good long term financial decisions.

Begin with the end

Setting financial goals and priorities isn't as hard as you might think, but you can also run into some surprising issues. For example, one exercise is to close your eyes and imagine yourself 'retired'. What does that mean to you? Where do you live? What activities are important to you? Imagine your retirement from what kind of car you drive to how often you visit your family.

Sometimes – in fact, more frequently than not – if I ask both spouses to do this exercise and write down their idea of retirement, they are vastly different. This is because they haven't really talked about it in detail; they just have this vague idea that they will 'retire' at a certain point but they haven't planned beyond that. When you are setting your financial goals and priorities, one of the most important aspects is getting everyone on the same page. There is no way to make a comprehensive plan if everyone wants something different.

Spouses aren't the only ones that need to get on the same page sometimes. I help families with multi-generational financial plans. That means that I develop a plan for money and assets to transfer from one generation to the next. Believe me there is nothing that can cause more heated arguments that trying to decide who gets what when mom and dad are gone!

Few families sit around and discuss finances or even really know where each other stand financially at all. They may have general idea, but no real clue as to the various assets or investments behind the scenes. They may also be shocked that things aren't the way they assumed. More than one grown child has left a family financial meeting angry when they discover that mom and dad aren't quite as wealthy as they thought and their share may be smaller than what they were counting on.

For this reason I encourage and help facilitate family money meetings. As children age it is important for them to know how to handle investments and how to plan long term. You might think that just because a person is raised in a wealthy environment that they would know all that, but it's not so. In fact, children of wealthy parents are much less likely to understand wealth management because they always had a parent or someone else that took care of it so they often weren't exposed to even the most basic concepts.

For this reason, my wife and I as parents, started early with the understanding we want to provide not only financial support for our children, but education that would benefit their own ability to plan their future. One of the main purposes of life insurance is for income replacement. I do agree. We were all babies once. Babies grow up and will eventually have an income that needs to be replaced in the event of their premature death. Does it make sense to purchase a life insurance policy for a 1 year old child? I believe it makes a lot of sense and did so for my children. This decision was made using a multi-generational wealth management planning mindset. The insurance isn't for me. The insurance is to guarantee their insurability forever regardless of any health changes as they grow.

My wife Tina and I wrote this letter to each of our children that we put on the cover of their whole life insurance policies:

Dear Johnny,

Mommy and Daddy love you more than anything else in this world. You are our legacy. We want to help you plan for your legacy one day and this policy is our gift to you.

Johnny, you are now only 2 years young. Mommy and Daddy purchased this policy for you because in the eyes of Manulife Financial, you will be a healthy and happy 2 year old forever!

Love you forever and always,

Mommy & Daddy XXOO

I hope I'm still alive one day to transfer the ownership of these policies to my children when they become parents and I become a Grandpa. I will then discuss with them how valuable these policies are and encourage them to do the same for their children some day.

As you can imagine, I spend a great deal of time educating clients and their families on wealth management strategies. This is one of the aspects that I love so much as it allows wealth that one generation created to be cared for by the next, rather than squandered or spent on a series of poor investments simply due to a lack of knowledge.

Part of this education includes the fact that you can't just set a plan and forget it. Your wealth must be managed to match your change in life from working to retirement to estate planning and so forth. Often people have multifaceted needs and so they must also have multifaceted goals and a multifaceted plan. In order to meet those goals you have to look at the reality of now and then be willing to adjust your goals and plan over time as that reality will change.

There are many transitions in life and the plan you need for the next five years will differ greatly from the one you need 20 years from now. This makes sense to people, but here again you'd be shocked how many millionaires I meet who haven't had a real in-depth financial review in more than a decade. No matter how long it's been, you have to start a plan with the end in mind, so determining your goals – and their priority - is an essential first step.

If you are relatively young and still have children at home, then things like a college education are going to rank high on the list. If you are an empty nester, retirement may be looming large on your horizon. As you transition to later years, you will be more concerned about being sure family is taken care of after you are gone and what kind of legacy you want to leave. All of these financial goals are important, but they will shift in priority over time and some will drop off completely as they are accomplished.

Thinking Long Term

When we start to think long term, almost everyone's mind goes immediately to retirement. Retirement planning is the process of determining retirement income goals and the actions and decisions necessary to achieve those goals. Retirement planning includes identifying sources of income, estimating expenses, implementing a savings program and managing assets. Future cash flows are estimated to determine if the retirement income goal will be achieved.

In the simplest sense, retirement planning is the planning one does to be prepared for life after paid work ends, not just financially but in all aspects of life. The non-financial aspects include such lifestyle choices as how to spend time in retirement, where to live, when to completely quit working and many other considerations. A holistic approach to retirement planning considers all of these areas because you can't make a valid plan in a void or without full information – that would be guessing.

The emphasis one puts on retirement planning changes throughout different life stages. Early in a person's working life, retirement planning is about setting aside enough money for retirement and the younger you are the less important this seems.

During the middle of an individual's career, it might also include setting specific income or asset targets and taking the steps to achieve them because you can see that time is winding down. In the few years leading up to retirement, financial assets are more or less determined, and so the emphasis changes to non-financial, lifestyle aspects and the specific steps to transition to that lifestyle.

There is a lot of worry about retirement because it plays out and affects everyone differently. There is also a very high chance that things will change by the time you get there so some of the assumptions you make today will not be exact. You may want something a little different than first imagined, or you may find yourself in a different life situation such as being unexpectedly single due to the death of a spouse. The whole idea of a plan is to allow you to grow your assets enough to give you options; it's not about setting those options in stone 20 years out and sticking to them no matter what. That's the great thing about a plan that is frequently reviewed because it is flexible and can keep up with not only variances in income but also with changing life situations.

I frequently hear the ideas of retirement and estate planning muddled together and it creates a lot of confusion. Even the media frequently intertwine the two so it's important that we define them separately here. Estate planning is a process involving the collection of preparation tasks that serve to manage an individual's asset base in the event of their incapacitation or death, including the bequest of assets to heirs and the settlement of estate taxes.

A comprehensive estate plan, with your Will as a key component, is one of the most important things you can do for the family members, friends and charitable organizations that you want to benefit from your estate. It can help enhance your wealth, minimize taxes, give your beneficiaries the greatest benefits, and ensure that your wishes are carried out as you intended.

There are many different tools used in estate planning that most people aren't overly familiar though they may have heard of them. Things like charitable remainder trusts, living wills, durable powers of attorney, and business succession plans can all be part of a good estate plan.

These are just a few of the tools available but that doesn't mean you need them all or that they will benefit you. Your plan will be different from your neighbor's or even your business partner's because you will each have different goals.

There are many aspects to creating an overall plan and you can't just do one part and leave the rest. That is why it is so important to find a trusted wealth advisor to walk you through the steps and educate you with the tools that may be unfamiliar to you so that your plan can address every area.

We will go into more depth about estate planning in a later chapter, but for now realize that it should be part of any comprehensive financial plan for a high net worth individual and that is why you must bring your will and some other specific documents to your wealth advisor.

The Paperwork

Once you have settled on a wealth advisor, you must bring a wide array of financial documents and personal information to him/her to get the process started. Before beginning, I ask my clients to organize their financial documents, by completing this easy-to-follow checklist:

- Monthly Cash Flow Statement, see samples at end of chapter

Retirement Planning Documents

- Recent RRSP statements
- Employee benefits program
- Deferred compensation and stock option agreements
- Pension and profit sharing statements

Tax Planning Documents

- Tax returns & Notice of Assessments for previous two years
- Recent pay stub
- Estimated income taxes for current year.

Financial Documents

- Savings account statements
- Mutual fund statements
- Brokerage account statements
- Investment documents
- Loan documents
- List of stocks held outside of brokerages
- List of what's in your bank safety deposit box
- Partnership agreements

Asset Protection Documents

- Life insurance policies and statements
- Medical, homeowners and auto insurance policies and statements
- Disability, umbrella, and long term care insurance policies
- Annuity policies and statements

Estate Planning Documents

- Copy of your will, living will, powers of attorney documents
- Living trust deeds

Yes this is a lot of paperwork! But in order to create the best plan possible, it is necessary for your wealth advisor to review all the documents – not only to ascertain your true financial situation, but also to point out any issues with your will or other documents that might need to be altered to meet your stated goals.

I frequently work with my clients' tax attorneys, lawyers, insurance agents and many other professionals when building a long term plan. It's not uncommon for clients to not reveal their complete situation to one professional or another that they regularly deal with, but your wealth advisor must be aware of any strategies or plans that might inadvertently cause a conflict with your overall goals.

It's normal for most people with a high net work not to want to reveal all their financial information to someone. But there is no way you will get good advice unless you are willing to reveal everything. By only allowing a view of one part of the financial picture, it's much more likely that you will get a mediocre plan at best that has no real possibility of meeting your goals. Don't set yourself up for failure before you ever really start! Be ready to start the relationship with full disclosure.

The table on the following pages is a sample net worth sheet. Yours will vary somewhat but should follow the basic idea put forth.

Net Worth Statement

Assets	Current Value	
A. Liquid Assets		
Checking Accounts	$30,000.00	
Savings Accounts	$50,000.00	
GIC & T-bills	$0.00	
Cash value of life insurance	$213,000.00	
Money market mutual funds	$300,000.00	
Other (eg. money owed to you, tax refund)	$0.00	
Total liquid assets	$593,000.00	*(A)*
B. long term assets		
mutual funds (non-money market)	$431,000.00	
Stocks	$3,240,000.00	
Bonds	$1,300,000.00	
RRSPs/RRIFs/RESPs	$816,000.00	
Company pension plan	$648,000.00	
Other	$750,000.00	
Total Long-Term Assets	$7,185,000.00	*(B)*
C. Property Assets		
Principle residence	$1,200,000.00	
Vacation property	$550,000.00	
Other real estate	$0.00	
Vehicles	$80,000.00	
Jewelry/Art/Collectibles	$120,000.00	
Other (eg. furniture)	$0.00	
Total Property Assets	$1,950,000.00	*(C)*

Liabilities	Current Value
Mortgage (principle residence)	$0.00
Other mortgages	$0.00
Personal Line of Credit	$0.00
Auto loans	$0.00
RRSP loans	$0.00
Investment loans	$250,000.00
Credit cards	$0.00
Other loans	$0.00
Total Liabilities	**$250,000.00**

Total Assets *(A+B+C)*	$9,728,000.00

Your Personal Net Worth

Total Assets	$9,728,000.00
Less total liabilities	$250,000.00
Equals: your net worth	$9,478,000.00

Chapter 5

Retirement Isn't The End

Chapter 5

Retirement Isn't The End

After educating their children, retirement is the biggest financial goal and priority for most people but what does it mean for you? The idea of retirement for most of us is some vague idea or concept that we don't think about in detail. We just know we're going to need money for it, so it bears asking yourself how retirement will look for you and how you will be living.

No one really sits on the porch in a rocking chair the last twenty years(or more) of their life – instead they may travel extensively, start a business or second career (or third!). Often people just think they will need a big pile of money for 'retirement' but they really don't think far beyond to how that money will affect their lifestyle or how their life will flow once they transition from their career.

One thing is for sure; we are all living longer but that doesn't necessarily translate into more retirement planning. According to a recent survey by Statistics Canada, a couple age 65 has a 50% chance that one spouse will live to age 90. While only 6% of Canadians work past age 65, 71% have done no retirement planning! It is shocking to think about the fact that 1 in 5 Canadians living today will celebrate their 100th birthday. There are currently about 4,635 Canadians over the age of 100, and by 2031, it is estimated that Canada will have 14,000 centenarians! You may be one of them so your retirement may last longer than you think even if you wait to retire until age 65. We just don't know how long retirement may be so we have to plan for the idea that it may extend far beyond 20 years.

In your planning, it's important to factor in the need for income to last upwards of 30 years. Not only will this protect you should in case you are one of these lucky few who live longer than expected, but it will also give you more options if unexpected events arise.

One of the first places to start when thinking about planning your retirement is to ask yourself, "When you picture your retirement, what do you see?" With the first members of the Baby Boom generation currently in their 60s, it's a question that a lot of Canadians should be asking themselves as retirement is fast approaching for a large segment of the population. Even if your own retirement is decades away, it's still important to have some objectives set so you can take full advantage of the time you have to prepare.

When you retire, there is a dramatic shift in every aspect of your day-to-day life. Planning for the challenges and opportunities ahead can make the transition smoother and make your retirement years truly rewarding.

What is your retirement dream?

Take some time and think about the lifestyle and options you would like to have during retirement. I know it can be hard to project into the future, but it is important to think about retirement in real terms because you will be living it at some point. Having a clear vision of who you are and what you want is the first step on the path to making your dreams a reality. What do you see for your future? Here are four common goals:

A life of leisure. Your new schedule means you have time to enjoy your favorite leisure activities, which might include playing golf, gardening, and socializing with friends, as well as cultural activities you may have missed out on during your working years. A common dream involves travel abroad — perhaps a cruise around the world, stopping in at exotic ports of call that you've read about but never had time to visit. Or you may develop a hobby that you had little time for while you were working.

But understand that a fulfilling retirement won't be all about leisure. It's likely that you'll eventually want to take up activities that offer the opportunity to use your skills and experience, develop new talents, and continue to contribute to the world around you. It sounds great to think about retiring and not working, but the truth is that leisure gets old after a while and we all want and need to feel productive.

Volunteer work. Many people find it rewarding to do volunteer work after they retire. Two or three half-days of volunteering each week can provide the structure you're used to, while leaving you enough free time to pursue your favorite leisure activities.

You may get involved in an organization or activity where you can make a difference by sharing your hard-earned expertise, perhaps through mentoring young people. You may work with the homeless or deliver meals to the elderly. There are as many ways as you can imagine to contribute and this can offer an excitement and fulfillment that is beyond any of your expectations.

A second career. An increasing number of people are choosing to use retirement as a springboard to a new career. Perhaps your idea of a fulfilling retirement includes starting a small business, or part-time work, such as consulting or teaching. Not only can you benefit from the activity, sense of accomplishment, and structure — there's the extra income to look forward to which can add to your options. So even if it may seem too late to put aside a more substantial amount for retirement, continuing to work even part-time can extend the retirement fund you do have. A friend of mine met a man in Florida while they were vacationing. He owned a dive instruction school but had previously been a banking VP at a large financial institution. After he retired, he traveled around the world diving in some in some of the most beautiful waters in existence. He was passionate about diving and soon opened the dive school so he could help other people experience what he loved so much.

Continuing education. Retirement is also a great time to go back to school and study subjects that interested you but were not in line with your chosen career. It can be the perfect opportunity to rediscover the joy of learning for its own sake. There are many seniors who take continuing education classes on photography, foreign languages, flying and even cake decorating. For example, I know of a woman in her late 60s who took a class on floral arrangements. For most of her life she was a high level government human resources director, but now she works part time in a local floral shop creating beautiful arrangements and she loves it.

Setting the foundation for your future

While many of us realize that turning retirement dreams into reality takes planning, far fewer actually take the necessary steps to make those dreams reality. The financial challenges of everyday life — the expenses of raising children, saving for their education, or paying down the mortgage — can make it difficult to focus on building retirement wealth. But that doesn't mean you can pretend like retirement is way down the road. It is a huge financial concern, but in order to start making progress you have to determine how big a financial concern it is for you and what you specifically will need to do to get there.

Ask Yourself:

How much income will you need to finance the retirement you want?

How much wealth will you need to generate that income?

What are the investments that will provide the growth and security that you need?

These aren't exactly easy questions to answer off the top of your head. Financial advice can help you establish realistic retirement goals and map out an investment strategy to reach your objectives that can work within your current lifestyle. That's an important part of creating a financial plan that will get you there.

Learning about the investment world and retirement planning isn't complicated. However, most Canadians don't take the time to learn about their options. Others just don't like to think about growing old. When it comes to preparing for the golden years, I don't engage my clients in conversations about retirement savings. Instead, I discuss lifestyle planning with them. This includes not only talking about what their future looks like in real terms but also debunking some of the common retirement myths.

There are many myths about retirement and the most common one is that everyone retires at 65. The truth is that there is no magical date for retirement. Some professionals and business owners want to work as long as they can. They want the option to work because they want to and not because they have to. These people enjoy the peace of mind that comes with financial security. Other individuals want to retire in their 50s and perhaps pursue second careers or other interests while they are still relatively young. Still others want to be prepared in case they are downsized or have to stop working for health or personal reasons. I know a 78 year old Dentist with the energy and drive of a 15 year old! He still takes care of his patients during the week and has a dentist chair at home for weekend emergencies. When he's not helping his patients, you'll find him cycling far distances and cross country skiing. He's a true inspiration and a role model. He has his supper most nights at 10pm! He's having too much fun to stop and eat! I can tell you that he will never retire in the traditional sense of the word; he is passionate about his work and that means it never feels like work.

I also remember one of my colleagues and friends who I worked with. Bruce was diagnosed with Lou Gehrig's disease when he was 39. He was given 3-5 years to live and chose shortly after his diagnosis to retire to share all his time with his wife and two sons. These trials in life do happen unexpectedly and because Bruce was well on his way as far as his retirement plans he was financially able to spend those precious few years with the people that really mattered. We all miss Bruce and his presence.

You and your mate may have very different ideas of what retirement looks like. For example, I have a retired married couple enjoying their early retirement years very differently. He is a retired mining company executive who lives in Monaco for six months of the year and spends most of his time sailing on the Mediterranean Sea. She is a retired geologist who lives in a condo in Napa California while her husband is at sea. She enjoys her time at a vineyard sampling wines and taking people on wine tours. They enjoy the other half of the year together back home surrounded by their family and friends. This has been their lifestyle since retiring in 2006.

Many couples never really talk about the details of their retirement dreams so it's common for them to have very different ideas of what retirement looks like.

Discussing your wishes sooner rather than later can help ensure that your financial situation will be able to fulfill both of your needs and dreams. Life goals and financial goals often go hand in hand. That's why it's important to have a clear idea of what you envision for your retirement, particularly as you make life-changing decisions along the way. Here are four key areas to consider, along with a checklist of questions that can serve as initial conversation-starters or points to ask your financial advisor to ensure that your retirement plan is in line with your retirement vision.

1. **Your lifestyle**

    How do you envision your lifestyle? If you expect to travel extensively or pursue costly leisure activities, your financial plan and savings strategy will need to take this into account.

    Have you discussed your plans with your partner? Be sure to openly discuss your plans with your partner, particularly if you are retiring at different times. Sometimes one spouse will retire while the other continues to work and this can be a strain which must be anticipated and planned for.

    Which activities will you pursue together and which will you pursue independently? How about the example I discussed above about the retired married couple sharing 6 months together and six months independently?

    This is a very creative solution that met both their needs and wants. By planning in advance you can find creative solutions that suit your needs as well.

2. **Your home**

What is your home worth? The equity you may have built in your home could represent a valuable financial resource that could be tapped into through a home equity loan or through downsizing — financial advice can help you decide if this might be appropriate for your situation. It is very important to remember that retirement isn't a one size fits all proposition so this may or may not be an option for you. Each situation must be looked at fully first and matched to your overall goals. You can get a sense of your home's value by checking the assessed value on your property tax form, investigating selling prices for comparable homes in your area, or requesting an assessment from a realtor. However, there are no guarantees that your home will be worth the same amount at the time you might decide to sell and here again you should only do so if it is in line with how you want to live in the future.

What is the emotional worth of your home? Moving from your home can be emotionally difficult, especially if you've raised you family there and developed strong ties to the neighborhood — so it's not an option for everyone.

3. **Your career**

Do you plan to start your own business? Starting a business may generate an income stream, but you'll probably need start-up capital. It can be well worth seeking financial guidance to help you ensure you are financially well-prepared for your new venture is this is the path you are looking at for your retirement.

Do you plan to continue working? Maybe you want to stay in your current job beyond the traditional retirement age or work part-time — for personal fulfillment or financial reasons. The longer you work, the less money you'll require to finance your retirement and the longer you'll have to save.

Is your employer open to phased-in retirement? You may want to consider a partial withdrawal from the workforce, during which you continue to contribute to a workplace pension plan while receiving pension benefits. I know a nurse named Nancy who was the nursing director at a small hospital. She wanted to partially retire and so she discussed these plans with her employer.

They were open to the idea because they recognized how valuable her experience was to the hospital. She worked part time for two more years and now still consults with her former employer on an as-needed basis. This has worked well for everyone involved and allowed her to transition from her career without feeling as if she abandoned her former calling. It also allowed her to continue to earn money while enjoying several years of semi-retirement.

4. **Leaving a legacy**

Is leaving a family legacy important to you? Perhaps you want to provide for children or grandchildren. Or, if you have dependants, such as minor children or disabled adults that you care for, discuss the possibility of setting up a testamentary trust in your Will.

Do you want to leave assets to charity? There are tax-effective ways to leave assets to charity, some of which can generate tax benefits during your lifetime. You may want to look at these now if charitable contributions are important to you.

Do you have a Will? No matter what your goals, you'll require a Will to make your wishes and instructions clear for your family after you are gone. Without one, your assets could be divided according to provincial or territorial law which may rob your family of income they could have had.

How Much Money Will I Need in Retirement?

Retirement represents a new phase in your life that has emotional and financial implications. The first step towards financial preparedness for retirement is to determine the amount of retirement income you will need. Conventional wisdom which suggested that you replace 60 – 70% of your pre-retirement income is now largely replaced by the realization that there is no infallible benchmark: how much you need in retirement depends on a number of factors, discussed below.

Ask yourself these questions:

Where will I be living?

Will you be staying in your current home? Or are you contemplating downsizing to a smaller residence to increase your retirement fund? Is moving from a big city to a less expensive part of the country in the cards? Are you hoping to spend part of the year in warmer climates? I have several clients who head south to their winter homes in Arizona and Florida to escape the harsh winter months in Canada.

Many of them will call or email me to let me know what they're doing in the winter months while I'm shoveling 5 feet of snow from driveway and hoping my car starter works so I don't have to get into a frozen vehicle!

The topics of reading on the beach, fishing, golfing, cruising and siestas are often mentioned and if you think this is a lifestyle that you want for your retirement, then you must take it into consideration when doing your calculations. I also know some folks who have moved from monstrous homes in the big city to a smaller quieter suburb or to live in their cottages year round. Their main focus is peace and an unassuming lifestyle so they can plan on a more scaled back retirement.

What activities will you pursue?

Do you envision travelling a lot or taking up new hobbies? What will be the estimated price tag be? Do you plan on becoming a "working retiree"? Today's retirees are more youthful and enjoy better health than ever, and some have decided to keep working for a few more years after retirement to fulfill social and emotional needs.

The decision to work part-time will also have a positive impact on your retirement income calculation. For example, one of my clients built a very successful car dealership during his career. When he decided to retire, he sold the dealership to some of his employees. He now uses his investment income to fund his retirement lifestyle. In his backyard, he built a huge winterized wood working shop with all of the wood working tools and machinery you can imagine. He can even live in this shop if he wants! He absolutely loves making custom kitchen cabinets and outdoor lawn and patio furniture. His passion has developed into a small business in his own backyard which provides even more additional retirement income.

Costs that change as you retire

Personal spending patterns

Once retired, you will likely be spending less on things like clothing and transportation. You may also no longer have a mortgage. On the other hand, you may be taking up new hobbies and activities and incur more entertainment and travelling expenses. You may also increase spending on medical issues and prescription costs. It's not that you will necessarily be spending less overall, in fact it may surprise you that you will probably spend more especially at first. Though that spending will shift, the tendency for most newly retired people is to cram in everything they want to do those first couple of years. So they travel extensively, spend time with family and even help their children financially. They may also move to an area (like Florida) where their cost of living is higher so even the mundane jug of milk costs more. Usually after those first couple of years, retirees have experienced a lot and settle into a more inexpensive lifestyle, but when the retirement fund takes a big hit those first few years, it may not have the ability to grow over time like you expect. For this reason you must prepare for the unexpected expenditures so you can enjoy your new retirement phase and not feel trapped in one place by finances.

Taxation

Your tax bill will likely go down when you retire. Moving to a smaller dwelling may also mean a smaller property tax bill. Depending on your retirement income sources, you may be able to take greater control over planning your taxes and benefit from various income splitting opportunities to lower your overall household tax bill. Income splitting is not an easy strategy to accomplish in Canada. We live in a tax system where every individual must report their personal income and pay tax esindividually. Income splitting is a strategy where couples try to move income from a spouse in a higher tax bracket to a spouse that is in a lower tax bracket. The government has been tough on income splitting because it would mean much lower tax revenue. For example, an individual who makes $140,000 per year would pay considerably more tax than a couple that earned $70,000 each.

An individual earning $140,000 in Ontario in 2011 owes $46,130 in combined federal and provincial income taxes. A couple that earns $70,000 each owes $15,986 respectively in combined federal and provincial income taxes. The net benefit in this example is an additional $14,158 after tax dollars for the couple to enjoy with splitting pension income provided they have pension income to split for tax reporting purposes. This example assumes there are no tax deductions or tax credits to report. Splitting pension income is one example that is of interest to retirees and great news for senior couples. The bottom line is that it doesn't matter how much money you earn. What matters is how much you keep after taxes. After all, income taxes are by far the biggest annual cash outflow for my clients. Canada has a progressive income tax system - the more you earn, the higher the rate of tax that you pay. Income splitting is a family tax planning technique designed to shift income from a high rate taxpayer to a lower rate taxpayer such as a spouse or children.

Contributions to pensions and savings plans

Pre-retirement expenses associated with contributions to public pension plans, employment insurance, employer pension plans and retirement savings (e.g. RRSP), will be eliminated. In fact, rather than saving, you now have the ability to draw on these income sources. So instead of outflow, it is now inflow which adds to your retirement money.

Health coverage

Your medical and dental costs could increase if you are no longer covered by an employee plan. I have some clients who are paying $1,000 + every month out of pocket for medication and treatments so this is a big consideration because most people will not have perfect health for their retirement years. Even a relatively small issue can grow as far as cost and you must plan for this fact of life.

Family Situation

People are living longer today, and many retired people have to also take care of their elderly parents. At the same time, this "sandwich generation" may still be providing financial support to their children, as young people stay in school longer and tuition costs skyrocket. Even adult children who lose a job or experience a divorce may be forced to return home (kids in tow) to live with Mom and Dad at least for a while. This dual responsibility may translate into unforeseen costs in retirement.

I have a family of clients that are experiencing this sort of family situation change. Eugene and Katherine were married for 58 years. In 2004, at the age of 83, Eugene passed away. His wife Katherine, who is now 87, was left with pension income totaling $1,800/month for the rest of her life. There were no other assets. They have one child, Norman who is now 62 and a retired school teacher on a fixed teacher's pension of $3,900/month. Norman is a widower with three children.

Katherine now has Alzheimer's, lives in a nursing home and requires 24/7 care that costs $2,700/month. She moved into this long term care facility 3 years ago. The $2,700/month includes all expenses (food, medication, healthcare, semi-private room). Norman is paying the $900/month shortfall each month for his Mom that her pension does not cover. This has reduced Norman's monthly cash flow by $900 or 23% which in turn has affected his spending habits since he's on a fixed pension. He now only goes on a big trip every second year – which is not exactly how he imagined his retirement would be.

When people get sick, no matter how wealthy they are, the first priority is recovery. Financial concerns can add unnecessary and unwanted worry during an already stressful time. Thanks to advances in medicine, the chances of surviving a critical illness have improved significantly over the past few decades. Fortunately, the three major causes of death – heart attack, stroke and cancer – if detected early and treated immediately, now have a much higher rate of survival. In fact, according to the Heart and Stroke Foundation and the National Cancer Institute of Canada:

- More than 80% of heart attack patients admitted to hospital survive;
- 85% of stroke victims survive the initial event; and
- 75% of men and 77% of women who develop cancer survive.

Of course, surviving a critical illness is extremely good news – but it can also be costly. Patients may be unable to return to work for an extended period of time. Among other things, they may also be forced to:

- Retrain for another type of job
- Travel some distance to specialized facilities for treatment
- Hire help for housework and childcare
- Make modifications to their homes to accommodate disabilities. In severe cases, they may also require nursing services at home or in a long-term care facility.

I've had several clients suffer at least one stroke during their retirement years. The Heart and Stroke Foundation reports that almost 18,000 Canadians aged 30 to 59 are hospitalized each year following a stroke. One of my retired clients suffered a debilitating stroke, and didn't have critical illness insurance. He had to pay $27,500 in acute care costs after a four month stay in the hospital. Additional house renovations to accommodate a wheelchair also cost him thousands of dollars. Modifications were required in the bathroom, bedroom and kitchen to accommodate his needs. For example, he needed a lift to get up and down the stairs, rails and handles to take a bath, and some cabinets and shelves lowered. He also needed some doors widened and ramps built. He also requires the care of a nurse at home that comes with an hourly charge of $40, which all adds up very quickly. He made a partial recovery but has now adjusted to his new way of life. While he is continuing to recover, his expected costs have skyrocketed because he planned on being healthy and that didn't happen.

Similarly, for those needing long-term care in a private nursing home could cost between $30,000 and $84,000 a year. Government-run facilities are less expensive but may still cost $12,000 to $57,000 annually. I have some clients who live in these facilities and it is a large expenditure for them.

My clients have worked hard and made it a priority to plan for their future and relied on the expertise of their trusted advisors. Unfortunately, several clients have been diagnosed with a critical illness in their retirement years (cancer, Alzheimer's, MS, ALS and others).

Things like out of pocket medical expenses and travel costs have to come from retirement income sources. Early withdrawals could have tax consequences and selling investments earlier than planned may not generate the required or expected returns. These things may derail retirement income plans.

Other Factors

Are you retiring early?

The earlier you retire, the more money you will need, not only because your income sources must cover a longer retirement period, but also because your savings period is curtailed. The amount of retirement benefit you will receive from CPP / QPP may also be impacted, especially if you also decide to start receiving those benefits earlier. Members of registered pension plans who retire earlier will typically receive a smaller pension income, as a result of the fewer years of service accumulated and potential early retirement penalties.

Inflation

Last but certainly not least, don't forget to factor in the rising cost of living. For example, if your estimated after-tax retirement income need is $50,000 a year, an annual inflation rate of 2% will mean that you need over $90,000 in 30 years' time – and inflation is running well ahead of that figure right now. Remember the $20 jug of milk? Not only does inflation increase the amount of money you must save, it reduces the purchasing power of that income over time.

Some people think that the idea of working to build your retirement fund is to deny yourself the life you want to live now so that you can hoard enough money to live the life you want in the future. That's sounds like backward logic to me. This idea is surrounded by the fear of running out of money. The money and energy being hoarded could be put too much better use by creating ongoing sources of income that will continue for your entire life no matter what your age or health.

You can see from these lists that there are many varied and complex considerations that go into determining how much money you need for retirement. That is why when I see an article or news story that talks about how you now need $2 Million (or whatever number) to retire I shake my head. There is no way anyone can determine how much you specifically need to achieve the retirement dream you want to live unless they sat down with you, understood your goals, and factored in all the variables.

The good news is that you can get the advice you need to help your personal situation. It is never too late to make the most of the income and investments you have while at the same time being secure in the knowledge that you are taking the right steps toward your retirement goals. If you haven't made your plan yet, you can start right now. Once you have it in place you can finally stop worrying and start living!

Chapter 6

Handing Down the Wealth

Chapter 6

Handing Down the Wealth

After you have worked hard your entire life, you want to be sure that the wealth you have accumulated goes to the people who are important to you, such as your family, in the best way possible. It's estimated that 47% of Canadian Businesses and 32% of the US businesses will change hands by 2014, according to Statistics Canada. This means that not only must these business owners consider how to hand down their monetary wealth in an estate plan, they must also do some business succession planning.

Business succession planning is a must for any business owner, but it doesn't just mean handing over the reins to the eldest child as it once did in generations past. Now the business owner must decide if, on their retirement or death, they want the business to be sold and the money passed on or if they want the family to retain the business as a going concern. There are many options and there are also many considerations.

A business succession plan is a written strategy that allows you to protect your business as you implement your desires for its continuation while at the same time allowing you to transition into a different phase of life. It outlines, in detail, how your business is to be transferred to another owner-operator. When done properly, a succession plan can prevent potential difficulties and increase the chances that your business will continue to thrive.

Regardless of whether you're transferring the business to an existing partner, senior executive, or family member, a plan is the best way to make sure it ends up in the right hands and continues in the right direction. This means that a succession plan is not something that can be done hastily or at the last minute. You need to carefully consider who should run the business when you leave, then train your successors, plan your exit, and decide how to transfer business assets. Ideally, a succession plan should be formulated years before you retire.

Plan carefully

Here are some of the considerations that need to be addressed:

1. **Decide who is going to take over your business and its assets.**

Will it be family members, business partners, or perhaps a member of your management team? If you decide on family, determine which family members are interested in, or capable of, running the business. It may come as a surprise to some entrepreneurs that some or all of their children have no interest in the family business – even if they have grown up working there. Just because that business has been your passion and your baby for decades does not mean your children will feel the same. Often we see businesses started and made profitable by one generation, run into the ground by the next. Your children are not you and while you may want them to be passionate about what you have built they just may not be. The worst thing you can do in that situation is dump the business on them and think they will get it at some point. What usually happens is a great deal of family bickering which tears the fabric of the relationships apart and destroys the business. When you are planning a business succession, you have to step back from the emotional connection you have with this wonderful business you have grown. It is just an asset and one that should be used to enhance your life as well as your family's – even if the best course of action is to sell it to someone else at some point. As usual in this type of complex situation, communication is key. It is important to have frank and honest discussion with the people involved whether they be family or senior management or both.

There is a family in Texas that owns a well known steakhouse. When their father died, the business was left to the eight children equally. Some of the children worked in the business and some did not. Since all had an equal say it led to many battles about how the business was managed. Over time, two of the brothers ended up buying out most of the other siblings but not before the relationships were irreparably damaged. I'm sure that is not what their father had in mind. He was trying to be fair and be sure all his children benefited from his lifetime of work, but that is not what happened. A business cannot be run by committee most of the time – especially a family committee. It might have been better to give the business to those that were interested in the first place and then come up with an equitable cash arrangement for the others from the very start or simply sell it and make the cash payments equal for all children.

There are many options and ways to pass down a business, but truthfully most of them are quite messy so good family communication and understanding is essential if it is to work well.

2. **If you're not the sole owner, what arrangements must be made with partners and shareholders?**

Many business owners have partners or shareholders that may or may not include family members. It is important to clarify the intentions of all the partners and get those plans in place, otherwise two senior partners may end up running the business with the other partner's children or spouse which may not be the optimal situation.

When you think about retirement, first you have to decide when you want to retire because not only do you need to plan for what that transition will look like, so do your partners. It is very common for one partner's death or retirement to put a tremendous strain on the company as a whole, but the better you can plan for it the less stress everyone will experience. You must also explore, and discuss with a qualified advisor, the most efficient ways to transfer ownership and assets without incurring an unnecessary tax burden.

3. **What happens if you die before you're able to transfer the business?**

Many businesses use what is called a business continuation plan to prepare for this possibility. It puts instruments in place that will compensate your family while at the same time ensuring the remaining partners are able to continuing running the business without interruption. In a very simple continuation plan, insurance policies are put into effect that pay the deceased's family and then agreements are created that transfer ownership to the remaining partners – but there an innumerable number of variations on this idea and each situation is unique, requiring a specific and unique plan.

4. **Who gets control and when?**

It is very important to discuss control. It is hard for any entrepreneur to stand by and watch someone else run things in a way they may not approve of, but if you are going to retire then you must come to grips with the fact that you will have to let go eventually. Even if you stay on as an advisor or board member, it's important to understand that you are choosing to step back and you must allow new management to find their own way.

How to Fire Your Father

Not long ago I came across an article on Yahoo finance written by Mitchell Kaneff. He is the author of the book *Taking Over: Insider Tips from a Third Generation CEO*. Mitchell's father was the second generation to run the family business, Arkay Packaging. Mitchell started at the company sweeping floors as the age of 15. When he graduated college in 1989 he came back and started in the customer service department. Over the next seven years he worked his way up and in 1996 his father appointed him president of the company. Mitchell's father retained the CEO role and still made most of the decisions. Father and son had very different management styles and visions for the company's future. This caused a great amount of stress in the C-suite as well as with the employees. Over the next 9 years the company rocked along, but by 2004 things had clearly come to a head. The COO threatened to quit and Mitchell knew the time had come. He picked up the phone and fired his father. It was the hardest call he'd ever made, but instead of being upset his father told him that he was very proud that he'd had the courage to do it. Mitchell's father knew it was way past time for him to leave but had stayed more or less out of habit and emotional attachment to the business.

This example is unusual because often this situation can dissolve into a huge dysfunctional mess and the ones who really lose are the business itself and the employees. But it also illustrates that a business can be successfully handed down without destroying the family that built it.

Legal agreements

To put any sort of business succession or continuation plan in place, you must draw up legal agreements – it's not something that can be accomplished on a handshake. There are income, taxation and ownership issues at stake which all must be clearly defined for the good of everyone involved. These may include provisions governing who can assume your portion of the business and under what conditions. For example, they may give existing shareholders the right to buy you out. You may be able to institute a shareholder agreement with other shareholders that facilitates your succession goals. If you're in partnership, pay particular attention to agreements that are already in place, including "buy-sell" agreements.

Your succession plan should establish a timetable for key events: training successors, your retirement date, and transfer of ownership. It should also outline your "strategic vision" — how you see the company being operated after you leave, and the management roles individuals will play in the company.

The road to your completed succession plan is complex. That's why it's important to enlist the help of professionals. You may need to work with management consultants who specialize in succession planning, as well as tax professionals and lawyers.

You should also consider how your succession plan ties in with your estate plan. For example, if you pass along the business to one child, how will you fairly compensate your other children? Once you succession plan is in place, review it regularly. This is especially important when there are changes in your family or business circumstances — for example, marriage or divorce, a birth in the family, a material change in the business or its ownership structure, or a change in tax and business regulations.

Case Study – Business Succession

Allen, a 68 year old widower is the sole owner of a very successful second generation manufacturing business (HoldCo). His daughter works with him in the business. Allen's other 3 children don't work in the business. His situation: The operating company is valued at $21 million and has no debt; HoldCo has $6 million in fixed income securities and the balance of his personal assets total $15 million; he has established an Individual Pension Plan and a Retirement Compensation Arrangement, both of which are fully funded; there is adequate key personal insurance in place in the event of death, disability or critical illness.

Allens's objectives:

1. His first concern is to find a strategy that will enable him to transfer the business to Rachel and still treat his other children equally.
2. As an active and committed alumnus, he also wants to make a significant contribution to his university.
3. He wants to improve the cash flow within the HoldCo and reduce its fair market value to minimize the taxes payable on his death.

When tailoring business succession plan for Allen's business, I met with him and his other advisors (lawyer, accountant, insurance agent) several times over two years to conduct a comprehensive review of the business and his own personal circumstances. As a result of the process, Allen had decided to commit $500,000/year to ensure family harmony is preserved and that a lasting legacy is put in place. We then helped Allen to arrange a combination of a Corporate Insured Annuity, Estate Equalization and a Private

Giving Foundation to meet all of his needs. The other children will receive compensation equal to the estimated value of the business and Amy will assume sole ownership of the business through the Corporate Insured Annuity and Estate Equalization. The Private Giving Foundation will ensure that Allen's alma mater receives a significant contribution as well.

A Business Will

Business owners may designate what will happen to their house, their car and their boat, but a surprisingly large number of business owners fail to make out wills specifying what will happen to their most important asset – their business – if they die. As a result, many leave family members and employees in the lurch. Many business owners think it's something they're supposed to do when they're old and ready to retire, which, in my view, is too late.

I have seen what happens when an owner has no business will. Next thing you know, the business is being sold at a fire-sale price. There's no one to take control, nobody knows anything, nobody can sign anything, or sell anything, and it becomes a big mess.

I've helped several business owners who want to sell their established operations upon retirement. Unfortunately, I'm often called upon by grieving families to assist in unwinding practices after the sudden death of that owner. My phone rings in times of crisis. The results are usually twofold. There is an immediate drop in the value of the business, and chaos occurs for family, staff and advisers.

A business will says that 'In the event of my death, do these things...' and a sequence of events, such as appointing an interim president and manager, leaving a set of instructions behind about who to call and what to do, and also what possible buyers there might be for the company is vital and needs to be updated every year.

When I ask a business owner what would happen to their business if they were hit by the proverbial truck, chances are they will just stare at me and you can hear a pin drop. Most of the time, it never really crossed their mind. How often do any of us contemplate our own mortality and even when we do, how often do we think about the business we leave behind? Most of my clients are entrepreneurs who are excited and passionate about their work. It's not something that comes naturally to think, 'What would happen if I didn't come into work tomorrow?'

The contents of a business will can also help keep a company running if an owner suddenly becomes ill, incapacitated or is otherwise unable to stay in charge. This can happen to anyone at anytime with something as simple as a car accident. You have to recover so who will be minding the store?

I personally know business owners who have had a child die or their spouse has been in a health situation, and the business just takes a back seat, whereas if they had thought through the possibility of some of the challenges in advance, when it wasn't urgent, they could go to plan B that they already have ready and take away some of the stress.

In large corporations, presidents and CEOs are replaceable in a moment. In a family owned business or professional practices, the family is the business so we have to think ahead and map out a suitable strategy.

Chapter 7

Estate Planning

Chapter 7
Estate Planning

Estate planning is an essential part of wealth preservation. The whole idea of estate planning is that you are planning in advance for the transfer of all your property after your death in the most advantageous way and to preserve as much of that wealth as possible.

Your estate would include all types of property you own from real estate, cars, collectables or artwork, investment and savings accounts, and even the family dog. There are numerous reasons to employ estate planning even if your estate is small (less than $1Million) and should absolutely be used if your assets are more than that. Some of these reasons are:

- To pay as little asset transfer tax as possible thereby leaving more money to your heirs.
- Being able to choose exactly who gets what and that your wishes for your final arrangements are followed.
- To assign guardians for any individuals in your care that may need ongoing care such as a child or elderly parents.
- To provide for final gifts to charities or institutions near and dear to your heart.

Estate planners employ several legal documents or tools to accomplish the goals most important to you. These might include but are not limited to:

Will – every person should have a will no matter how small their assets may be. This legal document specifies exactly how your property will be divided after your death. It outlines your wishes and assures you and your heirs that those wishes will be followed. An Executor is assigned in this document and this person handles the distribution of your assets as outlined in you will.

Trusts – there are many different types of trusts but each one is a legal document that basically holds property on behalf of, or for the benefit of, a person or organization. This document names a trustee who manages the property or assets on behalf of the person or organization (called the beneficiary).

Powers of Attorney –there are also different types of Powers of Attorney, but this legal document appoints a person to handle your affairs if you are unable to.

It is important to note that in order to do any type of estate planning, the individual must be of age, in good health and not under significant emotional duress. Many an estate has been challenged because some thought the plan was made to take advantage of a person that was not mentally stable or ill and usually these claims are made with good reason. This happens more than you think as there are many who prey on wealthy elderly people. Even if you are considered by most to be mentally competent, if you leave some outlandish provisions in your estate plan, then it will probably be challenged.

A notorious example of this is the troubles encountered by legendary heiress Leona Helmsley. With an estate totaling over $5 Billion she left most of the money to charity. But then she had one provision that created a trust for her little Maltese dog, Trouble. It was trouble indeed because when she created this will and trust she also cut out her grandchildren from benefiting from her estate at all. They got nothing. Of course they challenged the estate with the argument that no sane person would leave $12 Million for the dog. The judge agreed and the grandchildren received $6 Million to share plus legal expenses - the dog still got $5 Million! The lesson shows that if you are cutting people out of your estate they may have an argument a court will agree with – especially if you leave $12 Million to the dog.

It is always a good idea to have your mental health certified especially if your estate is large (and you know your will may anger some people).

This is a simple process and can be done by an attorney administering a mini questionnaire. While this may seem an unnecessary step, people can go to extremes where money is involved and this just makes sure your wishes are followed with the least legal interference possible.

Key Elements to an Estate Plan

Many people are often surprised at all the legal documents that make up a good estate plan, but when they really consider all the decisions that must be made when someone dies or becomes incapacitated, it makes sense. For example who gets what? What kind of funeral arrangements would you want? Who is in charge of the children? Who makes health care decision if you can't?

As you can see there are many decisions that are very difficult to make if your loved ones don't know your intentions and leaving them to sort it out can seriously diminish what you have worked to build your entire life.

Things that every estate plan should include are:

- Will (and possibly a trust depending on need)
- Letter of Intent
- Powers of Attorney (durable and heath care)
- Guardianship (only if needed)
- Estate Professionals!

The will and trusts will designate your beneficiaries, but these documents as well as all financial documents must be reviewed by a competent estate planner in conjunction with your attorney. The reason being you don't want to designate a beneficiary on a life insurance policy, for example, but then in your will assign that asset to a different beneficiary.

That will cause a challenge to your estate so everything must work together and be reviewed to be sure there are no inconsistencies.

As I already stated there are many different and varied trusts but one of the most common in estate planning is what is known as a testamentary trust. This type of trust separates management of the money from the person who will benefit from that money and there are numerous reasons this might be necessary such as for benefit of a child or disabled individual, spend thrift children, or even marital breakdown and divorce. It might also be used to help lessen the tax burden. Following are a few common examples.

1. **Beneficiaries in high tax bracket**

Mrs. Rich, an 80 year old widow has an only child Frank, a doctor who is in a 46% tax bracket. Frank has two daughters, Amy and Beryl, who are in their teens. Mrs. Rich has amassed $1 million of assets; her lifestyle is adequately funded by her regular income sources and in all likelihood, Frank will inherit the $1 million.

Frank is a high income earner and has no immediate need to touch these funds in the event that he inherits the money. Mrs. Rich can leave the estate to a trust for the benefit of Frank, Amy and Beryl. Frank can be one of the trustees. The trustees will confirm each year the allocation of income, so as to take advantage of the federal basic personal amounts of each child and the graduated tax brackets of the testamentary trust.

2. **Second marriages**

Allie and Jesse are married and both have children from their previous marriages. Allie wants to leave her assets to Jesse upon her death. However, Jesse's children are not on good terms with Allie! The problem for Allie is that if she leaves all her assets to Jesse when she dies, the assets will eventually go to Jesse's own children upon Jesse's death leaving her own children with nothing. To avoid this, Allie can set up a testamentary trust, naming Jesse as the income beneficiary; and providing that, upon Jesse's death, Allie's estate will be transferred to her own children from her first marriage.

3. **Spendthrift beneficiaries**

Mr. Cotter lacks faith in the ability of his son, David, to manage money. Instead of making David the beneficiary of his life insurance policy, Mr. Cotter opts to take out a $1 million policy, naming his estate as beneficiary and providing in his Will for the insurance proceeds to flow into a testamentary trust that permits David to receive regular payments of capital and income spread out over a specified number of years. This type of trust is very common these days!

This is just one type of trust showing a variety of uses but there are many more uses and many more types of trusts.

The letter of intent does not replace a will but it can help with your intention for the use of an asset. For example, you may leave a large sum to a child in your will, but in your letter of intent you say that you intend for that money to go for your grandchildren's education. This allows them the option of using the money at their discretion but they are aware of your wishes. Sometimes if a will is challenged, a letter of intent will also help a probate judge decide what your true intent was. A letter of intent can also be used to note what you want your final arrangements to be.

Powers of attorney are very important because they allow for management of your affairs should you become incapacitated. There are two different kinds that are important to estate planning: durable and health care. The durable power of attorney allows for management of your assets, while the health care power of attorney allows for the health care decisions. Most people will want a spouse or significant other making health care decisions, but often that is not the best person to manage a substantial estate. They may appoint an attorney or other member of the family to handle the money. Each document can list a different individual and this is a common desire for those with both large and small estates.

Guardianship is very important for those who have children, disabled relatives who live with them, or elderly dependent parents. Along with guardianship should be the allocation of ample assets to help care for those dependent individuals. For example, you wouldn't want to assign guardianship for your children to a sibling but then not allocate any assets to help care for them. Various factors must be weighed with the help of your estate planner to be sure future needs of these dependents are taken into account and enough of your estate is allocated to care for those you love.

With fertility treatments advancing almost faster than law can keep up, it is also important to add who gets custody of any stored eggs, sperm or embryos (or if they should be destroyed) in the event of a spouse's death. This has become a larger issue as more and more couples where at least one spouse has a dangerous occupation – soldiers, police officers, and firefighters for example – are choosing to store embryos in case they are injured or even killed in the line of duty.

The last item on my list is the use of estate professionals. This is not a self serving item though I am certainly one of those professionals. There are many 'do-it-yourself' prepackaged documents out there today but there is no way they can cover your specific needs and often they are too general to be of any real use. But sometimes even people in the legal profession, who should know better, can fall into the trap of trying to do estate planning themselves which is a tremendous error.

For example, when Chief Justice Warren Burger died in the mid 1990s, his estate was worth an estimated 1.8 million dollars. Being a chief justice, with what is considered a relatively small estate, he decided to draft his own will. It consisted of a mere 176 words. It wasn't the brevity that was the issue, but the fact that he didn't understand estate tax law, nor did he understand probate law. His error ended up costing his family $450,000 in estate taxes that could have easily been avoided. In addition, because his self-made will did not specify and address certain transactions such as selling real estate, his executors were forced to go to court every time they needed to complete a transaction which a well drafted will would have addressed eliminating the need for court approval and the many court expenses.

It is important to remember that it is not just wealthy people who need to consider estate planning. Amy Edwards, a sonographer in Texas, knew she was going to die. She'd battled cancer for five years and at age 39 was given just a few months to live. She had a boy, age ten and a husband she was estranged from. Like most people Amy owned a home that was far from paid for, and lived off what she made. Her only real asset was a $500,000 life insurance policy from work. Amy wanted to ensure that her son would be cared for, but also wanted to know that her husband would not have control of the $500,000 she wanted set aside for her son's care, education and future. She drafted a will that created a testamentary trust for the life insurance money and named her mother as trustee with the money to go to her son at age 25. She gave custody of her child to her husband but also drafted a letter of intent for her mother to know how much monthly support Amy wanted to go for her son's care and what arrangements she wanted for her funeral. So even though Amy didn't have substantial assets while she was alive, the life insurance policy she wanted to be used for her son's benefit and she was able to make that happen.

Amy knew how long she had, but most of us don't so every person should have at the minimum a will no matter how young they are.

Common Estate Planning Mistakes to Avoid

1. **Review that Plan!**

   As with a strong financial plan, an estate plan must be reviewed in full on a regular basis, preferably once each year. This is because not only do our financial circumstances change frequently so do our families and relationships. We get married, divorced, and have those close to us pass away on occasion. You may look back at your estate plan and find that several beneficiaries you previously named have now passed on, or that guardianship of your children was assigned to someone who now lives half a world away, or that your plan still lists an ex-spouse as executor.

   Being human, we easily forget about this sort of thing as we go along through our daily lives, but it can bring tremendous unintended consequences and this is the biggest and most common estate planning mistake people make. In 2008, popular actor, Heath Ledger died at the age of 28. He had done the right thing by putting a will in place three years earlier, but the problem was that he never updated it. In that ensuing three years he had met Michele Williams and they had produced a daughter together which Ledger dearly loved. Upon his death, his estate was distributed to his original beneficiaries, his father and sister leaving nothing for his beloved daughter. Though his father stated he would care for Ledger's daughter, he did so only after other family members raised concern in the media. He may or may not take care of the little girl and that uncertainly for her future exists today all because Ledger didn't update his estate plan. This shows that it is no small thing to be taken lightly so put a review of your estate plan on your calendar each and every year to be sure your intentions are fully known should something happen to you.

2. **Getting Around a Will**

I'm always surprise by the number of people that think putting their children on their investment accounts or adding them to the title of property is a cheap way to get around a will. It isn't. Despite some of the costs that come with creating an estate plan, the benefits far outweigh the costs especially when you can avoid probate and lessen your tax load.

Even if you are not sure you need an estate plan, it is highly recommended that you meet with a qualified estate planner and attorney to assure you have the legal documents you do need in place. When you include assets such as real estate, most people's estates are much larger than they think because they are assuming that their estate just includes investments or money in the bank. They don't take into account life insurance, qualified retirement plans and other miscellaneous assets like vehicles or artwork. Do yourself a favor and get professional advice on what documents and plans are needed for your specific situation.

3. **Forgetting about Life Insurance**

Most people don't realize that life insurance is fully taxable and if not planned for with the use of a trust or spousal exemption may send more than half of those expected proceeds to the tax man. We often have numerous small life insurance benefits we don't think about. These may be included on your car insurance policy, work benefits or even various stand alone policies that we may have forgotten about. It is important to hunt down all these possible sources of proceeds so your plan will not leave anything subject to more taxation than necessary.

4. **Incorrectly Titling Property**

Property titles are important documents and their titles must match the movement of those assets. When you set up a trust, you must be sure to go through the additional administrative step to be sure the property is titled properly. This is another reason frequent reviews are necessary. If you add property, sell property or share ownership of existing property the titles must be altered to be sure they will flow to the proper entities without court involvement upon your death. In addition, I also recommend that you do not listen to your realtor on these matters until you consult with a professional estate planner. Those who are buying and selling real estate often have no idea the issues that incorrectly titled property can bring into an estate situation so if you have an estate plan and add property, consult your planner before the purchase to ensure it will be titled correctly. This will save you the cost and hassle of having to re-title it later.

5. **Incorrect Beneficiary Designations**

This is also quite common and the most frequent issue in this area is designating minor children as contingent beneficiaries on their parent's policies. In the 1990s a young couple, Jennifer and Lupe Renteria were returning home from a family gathering on Valentine's day. They had two small children ages 5 and 7. They had wills that designated that in the event of both their deaths, a testamentary trust be created to administer the life insurance funds (policies of $400,000 each) until the children were 25 because they saw the danger of allowing an 18 year old to suddenly have a large sum of money at their disposal.

Unfortunately they were involved in a terrible traffic accident and while the children escaped with only minor injuries, both parents were killed. Unfortunately, the parents had named the children as contingent beneficiaries on the life insurance so the law dictated that the policy be followed and the children received the money at age 18 – the complete opposite of the parent's intention.

While this is an extreme example, I have seen similar situations happen many times so it pays to have an estate professional check any and all beneficiary designations.

6. **No Disability Planning**

No I don't mean disability insurance, although that is part of an overall financial plan. In terms of estate planning people frequently assume they will be healthy with all their mental faculties right up until the day of their death, but we know that is often not the case. You must plan for the fact that when you die you will have some sort of diminished physical or mental capacity or both. This means that you may live months, years, or even decades with someone else managing your assets and your long term care – and don't assume your spouse will be there to take care of everything. Odds are they will not be there or if they are, may exhibit a similar diminished capacity and in no way be able to care for you. It is import to sit down with your estate advisor and work through these what ifs to ensure you have contingencies and backups in place should your health or capacity come into question.

7. **The Half Effort**

By far the greatest danger to your estate is procrastination. It is easy to put off planning but you must realize that by doing so you are jeopardizing everything you have worked for or will work for. If you do decide to make an estate plan, don't just go to a run of the mill accountant or attorney or financial advisor. Laws and taxation governing estate transfers are very complex and estate plans must be equally complex to properly address various issues. You need a number of various professionals in your life to coordinate your plan and work together. These include your estate planning advisor, insurance professional, tax accountant and attorney. The reason it is important to have all these people is that they each bring a different perspective to the mix. The accountant knows the ins and outs of tax law, but not probate. The lawyer may know probate but not tax law. Your estate planning professional can spearhead and coordinate everything from re-titling assets to match the trust documents, to being sure beneficiary designations are correct. You can't give your plan half effort or you will achieve only part of the results you want, exposing your estate to exactly the kind of risk you are hoping to avoid.

Sample Case

Following is an example of an estate plan such as the ones I help create every day. This shows exactly what can be accomplished with the right planning.

Estate Planning Case
The Hickey & Svalina Wealth Management Group

These clients represent a large multi generational family owned industrial business. When we first engaged them, they had not addressed any of the complex issues that face clients like these. Below are the relevant points that led to a comprehensive solution that was implemented for them.

Client Description:

- Net worth in excess of $52,000,000
- Five Family Shareholders
- Large Capital Gains in Company
- Father has used his $500,000 Capital Gains Exemption but the others have not. Capital Gains Exemption has since been increased.
- No Succession Plan in place
- No Insurance in place
- Children who were shareholders were not married but may someday
- Estate Freeze done 10 years ago. The business has since enjoyed tremendous growth
- Company is cash and asset rich
- No one was addressing these issues!

Process Followed:

- Obtained permission and relevant information from the client to proceed
- Formed relationships with their 2 accountants and their lawyer
- Brought in our EPA (Estate Planning Advisor)
- Brought in 2 outside Tax Lawyers

- Developed a Credible Timeline
- Worked for 1 year with accountants and lawyers until we had all the current and relevant data

Results Generated:
- Updated their *Personal Wills* to include provisions for *Testamentary Trusts*
- Introduced the concept and implemented *Business Wills*
- Formation of *Shareholders Agreement*
- Issued *Preferred Shares* to Mother (so she could take advantage of what was then a $500,000 Capital Gain Exemption)
- Issued *Common Shares* to Children (so they could each take advantage of what was then a $500,000 Capital Gain Exemption)
- Executed an $12,800,000 *Estate Freeze for Children*
- Calculated Tax Liability upon death
- *Insured all parties* from this tax liability upon death
- Creation of *Spousal Trusts* to facilitate the shares of the Mother to eventually go directly to the children
- This allowed for *Creditor Protection* and protection from *Failed Marriages*

Savings to our Client:
1. Testamentary Trusts =$ 10,000
2. Business Wills =$ 150,000
3. Mother as Shareholder =$ 500,000
4. Kids as Shareholders =$1,500,000
5. Estate Freeze =$ known later
6. Insured Tax Liability =$2,000,000
   Total Savings =$4,160,000

Chapter 8

Put Your Money Where Your Heart Is

Chapter 8

Put Your Money Where Your Heart Is

The idea of saving your money and accumulating assets is not only to benefit you in retirement but also to enjoy! This may include acquiring or utilizing a long held family asset such as a vacation retreat. During the summer months, many families spend time together away from the hustle and bustle of daily living and retreat to one of the "four C's" of summer: the cabin, condo, chalet or cottage. What's lurking under the surface of your idyllic retreat may be a host of tax and estate planning issues that, if not tackled early on, could not only cost you (or your heirs) a lot of cash, but in extreme cases, could force the sale of the recreational property that may have been in your family for generations.

Probate Tax Planning

One of the key functions of creating an estate plan, it to allow you to plan for probate tax. Upon death, each province (except Quebec) levies a probate fee on the value of assets passed through the estate. That probate fee ranges from 0.4% in Prince Edward Island to 1.5% in Ontario. For example, an Ontarian who wills her $500,000 Muskoka cottage to her kids would face a probate bill of about $7,500. In fact, without proper planning, a vacation property could be subject to probate tax twice: once on the death of the original owner and, if left to a spouse or partner, again on the death of the survivor.

Following are some common planning techniques that may be helpful to reduce or eliminate probate fees payable upon death. They include joint ownership and trusts.

Joint ownership

One common probate-avoidance technique is to register the title of the property in joint tenancy (each joint owner has an undivided interest in the entire property). This type of joint ownership with right of survivorship means that upon the death of one owner the property is simply transferred directly to the surviving joint owner, bypassing the estate and therefore, not subject to probate.

The advantage of joint ownership, however, is mired in a plethora of other problems, some of which may be more significant than the probate bill. The biggest problem, and the subject of two 2007 Supreme Court of Canada cases, is proving the transferor's true intention - was it a gift or merely an estate-planning strategy?

For example, say John transfers his $1-million Whistler condo to joint title with his adult daughter, Anna, whose family vacations there on weekends in summer and skis there for two weeks during Christmas. John's other child, Michael, lives in Halifax, and does not use the property at all. Upon John's death, the property will simply transfer directly to Anna's name, bypassing the estate and avoiding probate fees of $14,000 (at the 1.4% B.C. rate). But did John really intend for Anna to inherit the entire value of the condo, to the exclusion of Michael? What if the condo was the only major asset owned by John upon his death and there was little else left in his estate for Michael?

If the two Supreme Court of Canada summarized below are any indication of what might happen in this hypothetical example, Michael would likely hire a lawyer and sue his sister for half the value of the condo, arguing that the transfer into joint ownership was merely an estate-planning ploy meant to avoid probate. Surely, Dad didn't intend to disinherit Michael - or did he?

Cases from the Supreme Court of Canada - Joint Ownership

In May 2007, the Supreme Court of Canada released simultaneous judgments in two Ontario cases: Pecore v. Pecore (2007 SCC 17) and Madsen Estate v. Saylor (2007 SCC 18). What was at issue in both cases was the meaning of "joint ownership with rights of survivorship" (or JTWROS) of investment accounts and the true intentions of the original owners when the joint accounts were established.

In the first case, Edwin Hughes, father of Paula Pecore, put nearly $1 million of mutual funds into joint ownership with his daughter Paula. Upon Mr. Hughes' death, the assets in the joint account were transferred into Paula's name. Two years later, Paula and her husband, Michael Pecore, separated and, in the course of the divorce, Michael tried to go after the assets in the joint account since he was a beneficiary under his ex-father in-law's will. His argument was that the transfer of the joint account into Paula's name was not a true gift since it was done "for probate purposes only". Both lower courts disagreed and found that Paula legitimately inherited the account through JTWROS.

The second, very similar case, involved Michael Madsen who named only one of his three children, Patricia Brooks, as the joint owner of his investment accounts. After Michael's death, Patricia's brother and sister sued and claimed that their late father only named Patricia on the account "for convenience purposes" and thus no true gift was made. As a result, the monies in the joint accounts should be distributed in accordance with the will, with both siblings receiving a portion of the funds. Both lower courts agreed.

The Supreme Court of Canada (SCC) saw no reason to reverse either of these lower courts' decisions. The court found that due to the presumption of resulting trust, the onus falls on the surviving joint account holder to prove that the transferor intended to make a gift of any remaining balance in the account.

Factors that should be considered to determine the transferor's intent include:
- wording in a financial document used to open an account

- control and use of the funds while the transferor was alive
- whether a power of attorney was granted
- who paid the tax on the account
- any other evidence the court finds necessary to establish intent.

As a result of these two cases, it may be a good idea to document your intention when making your vacation property establishing a JTWROS. One way to do so is by signing a "Declaration of Intention" for joint assets. Legal advice is warranted here.

Trusts, including "alter-ego trusts"

Using trusts to hold vacation property can help to avoid probate fees upon death since property inside the trust is not included in the value of your estate. As discussed above, however, transferring the vacation property with the accrued gain into the trust could give rise to capital gains tax, which could negate the ultimate probate avoidance motivation.

That being said, if you are at least 65 years of age, you may wish to consider transferring the vacation property into an "alter-ego trust" or a "joint-partner trust", which can be done without having to pay immediate capital gains tax on the transfer. In order to be an alter-ego trust or joint partner trust, no one other than you (or you and your spouse or joint partner, in the case of a joint partner trust) can be entitled to the income and capital of the trust during your lifetime.

You can continue to maintain full control of the property through the trust, but you can name your children as the ultimate beneficiaries of the trust, who would then inherit the property upon your death.

Since at the time of death you no longer own the property - it's owned by the trust - it's not included in the value of your estate for the purposes of calculating probate tax. The downside, of course, is that there may be income tax consequences associated with the deemed disposition of the property upon death as the property is deemed to be disposed of inside the trust, which is subject to the top marginal tax rate.

U.S. Vacation Properties

In Canada, upon death, there is a deemed disposition of all your property at fair market value. Any capital gains tax resulting from accrued appreciation (from the date of purchase to the date of death) is payable on your final return. Not so in the U.S. where citizens and green card holders are taxed on the fair market value of all property owned on the date of death under the "estate tax" regime.

Even if you're not a U.S. citizen, the U.S. estate tax could apply to you if you own property in the U.S. upon death, which includes U.S. real estate. Estate taxes in the U.S. can be considerable amounts and it's a good idea to do some planning in advance.

Some other commonly used strategies to reduce probate fees:
- Holding property in joint name with right of survivorship (outside of Quebec). Numerous potential issues with this strategy as discussed above especially where the joint owner is not a spouse.
- Designating beneficiaries on registered accounts and life insurance plans.
- Creating *inter vivos* trusts.
- Making gifts during your lifetime.

Another interesting method for minimizing probate taxes in at least one province (i.e. Ontario) is the use of multiple Wills. To understand how this strategy works, let us first understand the probate process.

Why is probate required?

The main purpose of probating a Will is to validate the appointment of the executor (i.e. the person appointed in a Will to control and protect the estate's assets, pay off any debts and distribute property as directed by the Will).

Specifically:
- Probate may be required before a legal change in ownership of real estate property can be made.
- Probate can protect the executor and third parties from legal liability.

- Third parties (e.g. financial institutions) often require probated Wills before they will accept instructions from the executor named in the Will.

How does the multiple wills strategy work?

This strategy involves preparing two Wills, one dealing with assets administered by third parties such as bank accounts, investment portfolios and real estate; and another designed for personally held assets such as personal effects and shares of a private company. In Ontario, the use of multiple Wills is now accepted practice following the decision of the court case *Granovsky v. The Queen*. The judge in this case ruled that if a person dies with multiple Wills, the executor seeking probate is not obligated to probate all of the Wills. The executor has the option to probate whichever of the Wills of the deceased and probate taxes would apply only on the assets that were part of the probated Will. In other words, it is possible to segregate assets of an individual into multiple Wills:

- A primary Will holding the assets that require the probate process.
- A secondary Will holding the assets that do not require probate (e.g. privately held shares or personal properties).

The result is lower probate costs because only the assets of the primary Will are subject to the provincial probate tax. Let's look at an example to make this technique a little clearer.

George, a widower with no children, lives in Ontario and owns an incorporated small business. The privately held corporation is worth $500,000. George owns his principal residence which is worth $350,000 (no mortgage), a valuable collection of Group of Seven paintings worth $150,000 and he also has $100,000 in a non-registered investment account.

With one Will, George's probate taxes would amount to $16,000. But with multiple wills, the probate taxes would amount to only $6,250. Therefore, by using multiple Wills there is a probate tax savings of $9,750 ($16,000 minus $6,250)!

Probate tax planning can save significant amounts of money for your heirs or loved ones. This is particularly important if many of your assets aren't fluid – like real estate or business interests. If not properly planned for, the cash the family must come up with to pay these taxes may force the sale of your business, the family home or other assets that you intended for them to keep and benefit from.

Dependent Children tax considerations

We already touched on the idea of a testamentary trust to take care of young children, but to show how much this can possibly save in taxes, let's revisit the concept with an example. As we discussed earlier, a testamentary trust is created by your will and only takes effect on your death. The Trustee has discretion to distribute income and capital amongst your beneficiaries according to the directions in your will.

A Testamentary Trust gives your family both flexibility and control over when and how they receive their inheritance. Depending on your will, the Trustee may distribute the income or capital to Beneficiaries at various times and in differing proportions. The Testamentary Trust can be wound up at any time, or kept open for an extended period. Because the Trust Assets are not legally owned by your Beneficiaries, but rather by the Trustee, they are protected in situations such as legal proceedings, bankruptcy or marital breakdown.

The tax laws provide favorable treatment for beneficiaries of a Testamentary Trust who are under 18 years of age. In the case of a Family Trust (which operates during your lifetime) distributions to minor Beneficiaries are taxed at penalty rates. However in the case of a Testamentary Trust, minor Beneficiaries are taxed at normal rates.

Consider this example: Jane and Paul have two school-age children. If Paul dies, Jane will inherit $500,000. Jane works, and has a good income, so she pays tax on her income at the highest marginal rates. The expected income from this inheritance, calculated at 7.5% per annum will amount to $37,500. If Jane inherits in her own name then the tax on the additional income will amount to $16,125 leaving Jane with a disposable amount of $21,375 each year from the trust income.

On the other hand, if Jane inherits as Trustee of a Testamentary Trust in which she, Paul and their children are all Beneficiaries, she would be able to allocate the income to the two children who have no other income, and the income would then be taxed at the rate of $1,912.50 each for a total tax of $3,825.00 leaving disposable income of $33,675.00. This is an improvement in the amount of available cash *each year* of $12,300. As it happens, that is almost the same amount as Jane and Paul pay in annual private school fees for each child, so the effect of the tax saving is almost the same as having a full annual scholarship for one child.

Your Trustee will have wide discretion to retain and preserve income and capital of the Trust or to distribute it to a range of family beneficiaries. Because of the flexible nature of the Trust, the Trustee will be able to stream income to Beneficiaries who are likely to be taxed at the lowest marginal rates, thus minimizing the tax payable. Income, and also capital can be made available to Beneficiaries for a variety of purposes including education, setting up a business, buying a residence or meeting day to day needs and expenses.

Flexibility is at the heart of the arrangement to ensure that the Trust income and capital is used for the maximum advantage of the Trust Beneficiaries but without allowing their inheritance to get into the hands of family members who might not be of an age or maturity level to manage their own affairs yet.

One of the main benefits of this type of trust is that it separates the trustee from those who benefit – the beneficiaries. This provides protection from many types of risk, including but not limited to:

- family break-downs and divorce
- the challenges of blended families
- insolvency
- professional negligence
- drug and alcohol abuse and dependency
- being sued by vicious creditors
- the inability to manage one's own affairs.

A testamentary trust allows your family to achieve the best of both worlds. They have the ability to access the income and capital how and when needed but at the same time, their inheritance is protected by the structure set up in your will.

The following is another example of how this type of arrangement can both protect and provide for minor children:

James and Erica have a combined Estate worth $1,600,000. They have two young school-going children. James and Erica wish to ensure that in the event of their deaths, their young children will be provided for, although the children are not yet ready to manage or control their inheritance.

James and Erica's wills each create a Testamentary Trust which will only take effect on death, to ensure that their children are well provided for during their educational years, with the value of their inheritance continuing to be preserved until they reach an age when they can manage their own affairs.

Their will makes special reference to providing income for educational purposes, accommodation, maintenance, income and the like, giving the Trustee enough discretion to ensure that adequate income is made available for all these purposes.

When the children reach a pre-determined age, for example, age 25 (the age varies from one family to another), they may be given full or partial control of the Trust with the ability to either continue the Trust for tax and other purposes or to terminate it.

Disabled Children and Adults

Often disabled individuals receive some type of government assistance, for this reason it is very important to create an estate plan that provides for continued care and takes all the various factors of their care into consideration.

Canadians with a disability may receive monetary support payments from the government. However, in order to receive these funds the person must be deemed to be living in poverty. Each province has its own program to provide these payments. In Ontario for example, the Ontario Disability Support Payments (ODSPs) is the program that handles distribution of these funds. There are restrictions to the liquid assets that may be held by these individuals and if they suddenly inherit even a modest sum that puts them over these limits, they will be released from the program and have to reapply down the road when the money runs out.

It is clear that a caregiver would want the inheritance to be spread over that person's lifetime so in the 1980s something called a Henson trust was created.

This type of trust allows the property or assets to be the property of the trust and controlled by the trustee who has discretion on the amount used to benefit the beneficiary. This allows them the flexibility to meet the standards set by the Ontario Social Services Ministry.

Following are a few examples of clients who are considering a Henson trust. I've listed their family and financial situation and then also outlined the direction I would recommend.

Profile of two families considering a Henson Trust

Wealthy Family situation:
- A wealthy family with a child whose medical needs are not covered by ODSP (Ontario Disability Support Program) and the Ontario Drug Plan.
- Alana and David have a net worth of close to $4 million. Their $2.8 million investment portfolio generates $170,000/year of interest and dividend income.
- Their disabled 30-year-old only son, whose name is Henry, is employed while receiving an additional monthly amount from ODSP. He does not have many expenses apart from medical ones.

Henry needs prescriptions that are not covered by ODSP and the Ontario Drug Plan. He also needs orthodontic and mouth reconstruction therapies that are not covered by ODSP.

- Alana and David do not have any family members who could help administer a trust.
- Alana and David have had good legal and financial advice. Still, they are unsure about setting up a discretionary trust such as a Henson Trust. They do not understand all of the rules about ODSP. They worry that if their son continues to do well at his job, he may not qualify for ODSP in the future.

- Advice: Alana and David should consider planning their estate to take care of all of Henry's needs both current and future rather than setting up a Henson trust. The estate seems to be large enough to support Henry long term, and many of his healthcare expenses are not covered by ODSP and the Ontario Drug Plan anyway. When the estate starts to support Henry, he must withdraw from ODSP.

It would make sense to have the estate placed in trust if the parents are concerned that Henry will be unable to manage it himself.

Alana and David may want to consider a trust company to ensure that the capital is appropriately invested. Henry could be given a substantial monthly allowance to spend as he sees fit, if he is capable of managing these funds, so his independence could be maintained, while his long-term financial interests will also be protected.

Modest Income Family Situation
- Sally and Michael have an estate of close to $150,000 that has the potential to pay out $7,500 per year.
- Their 37-year-old daughter, Nancy, has schizophrenia. She does not have a job, and probably will never have an income from employment. All of her prescriptions are covered by the Ontario Drug Plan. Nancy needs special teeth cleaning that she can get through the ODSP special care dental plan.
- She cannot live on her own, and cannot live with her brothers and their families. Nancy's brothers are successful and well-established, and likely will not require support from their parents' estates, at least not for a long time.
- ODSP benefits are $12,000 a year plus the drug and dental program. Clearly, ODSP provides more than their estate could provide for Nancy's housing, food and other basic expenses. ODSP also covers all of Nancy's health-related costs.
- With Sally and Michael's estate, Nancy will have a yearly income that is well within what ODSP will allow. From the estate, Nancy could get about $5,000 a year in gifts and up to $2,500 a year for expenses related to her disability (such as payment to a support person).

- Advice: In this situation, a discretionary Henson trust is a very good option. Sally and Michael's estate is not large enough to cover all of Nancy's needs. By planning their estate accordingly, Nancy will continue to receive her ODSP benefits and the trust will just add a small amount that ensures it lasts as long as possible.

When thinking about setting up any kind of trust for the long term care of a mentally or physically disabled loved one, all factors must be taken into account and thoughtfully considered. There is no 'one size fits all' solution so don't assume that because someone else you know set up a Henson trust for their loved one, that you should too.

You first must get competent, qualified advice from someone that can review your entire situation before making any sort of recommendation.

Making the World a Better Place

Often, when a client is contemplating the scope of their estate plan, they have a desire to give to organizations and charities that mean a lot to them. It is a very common desire to leave the world a better place for you having existed and once your family is taken care of there is a great deal of good that can be accomplished through charitable donation.

Even something as honorable as giving money to a good cause must be planned for. You want the maximum amount to go to that charity and be used well, so setting up charitable trusts of one sort or another is key to ensuring that organization benefits the maximum amount.

I deal specifically with high net worth individuals and rarely is an estate plan created for them without some aspect of charitable donation. Following is an example of what can be accomplished by someone with a giving heart no matter their own situation:

In 2007, Mischa Weisz was diagnosed with terminal pancreatic cancer. His close friend and financial advisor, Frank, who frequently went far beyond assisting clients with their investments, was eager to lend Mischa a hand during his illness in any way he could.

A self-made millionaire, Mischa's life story reads like a movie script. He evolved from a single father of two, living on unemployment insurance in subsidized housing in Hamilton, to the founder of TNS Smart Network Inc., a company responsible for processing ATM withdrawals for 13,000 independently-operated Canadian bank machines located in places such as gas stations, stores and casinos.

When Mischa's health deteriorated, he sold his business, and with Frank's help, began to put his affairs in order. After providing for his family, charity was a priority in his overall estate plan. He left $500,000 to the Hamilton YMCA, to be used for children's community outreach programs. The Y was an obvious choice for Mischa, since he wanted to express his gratitude both for that institution's influence on his own life as a child, and for the tremendous benefits his children had gained from the Y's programming while he was a struggling single father.

He also made a $500,000 donation to the Juravinski Cancer Centre, where he was treated. That gift allowed for the purchase of Ontario's first Cyberknife Robotic Radiosurgery treatment option for cancer patients. It uses lasers and computers to pinpoint tumors deep inside the body and destroy them. This technology allows a level of precision that is not currently available for some cancer patients, especially for those who have tumors which are considered inoperable or surgically complex. Mischa had hoped this treatment option would be in a place to help him but when he learned his time was short, he simply wanted it available for future patients.

He also bequeathed $250,000 to Woodview Children's Mental Health and Autism Services to create the Mischa Weisz Centre for Autism Services, a unique facility that will provide services to children, youth and adults living with autism in the City of Hamilton.

The remainder of his estate (over $2 million) was left as an endowment fund with the Private Giving Foundation (PGF) in order to continue to support the causes that were important to him.

Mischa battled cancer tenaciously, and survived for nearly 25 months after learning he could expect to live for only five. He firmly believed that everyone has a duty to make something worthwhile out of their lives, and to help society in some way that people remember. This was evident by his generous legacy to the PGF, ensuring that funds will be available year after year to support the causes that were important to him, and that those closest to him will play a pivotal role in how those funds are allocated. His legacy can be summed up by the words he carefully selected for his tombstone: "As long as my name is spoken, I will still be alive."

Micha's story is an example of how the hard work you have engaged in during your lifetime can be paid forward to future generations allowing them to have a better life.

Chapter 9

Lost and Stolen Nest Eggs

Set For Life

# Chapter 9

Lost and Stolen Nest Eggs

There are numerous events that might cause you to lose your nest egg. These include such things as poor or ineffective planning, market disasters, natural disasters, personal disasters and just downright thievery. While you can't plan for every instance you can plan for many of the ups and down and maintain a healthy perspective.

Given recent economic events, I frequently talk to people whose net worth is a fraction of what it was just five or ten years ago. Many of the 'dot com' instant millionaires from the 1990s are now worrying how to pay their bills. Other individuals who spent their entire lives ascending to the executive level or building their own businesses have seen that security crumble as the economy struggles. There will always be downturns and you can't choose when they will happen, but there are few things you can't recover from financially.

The biggest obstacle that many people have in times of financial trial is that they either partially or fully equate their net worth with self worth and it's easy to do. You create grand plans of the trusts you will leave your children and the donations you will make to beloved institutions. You do everything right create your own wealth but then in a very short period of time it's gone or decimated to the point those plans are now moot. This creates a psychological double whammy. You can't help but feel like a failure simply because all your well laid plans and dreams are out the window. You wanted to contribute to the security and future of other people in your own family and those who would be helped by the money you donated. Now not only can you not help them, you can't even ensure your own future.

This goes back to the fundamental reason we create wealth plans in the first place – fear. Losing part or all of your financial security brings that fear roaring back to life and it can be overwhelming. You can't sit around and think that because your bank account is less than before that you are worth less as a person. Depression can easily set in and that just creates a downward spiral that can be very hard to recover from.

In order to get back on the road to recovery and get a grip on your financial future again, you must focus on the present. You must do those things that make sense financially right now. You can't lament over the money that doesn't exist anymore or the life you used to live. What you have now is the opportunity to start over and understand that your experience has offered valuable lessons that you have learned from.

As we talked about at the first of this book, perceived losses are felt more deeply than gains and while you may have been satisfied with your nest egg, losing even part of feels absolutely devastating. The only way to sooth that feeling is to take a broader picture. With my clients, I discuss the timeline they have to work with and put whatever losses they may have incurred into that wide perspective. When taken as a single event, the lost hurts worse but when seen in a longer view, it's just a bump in the road.

As you recover from the loss, it is good to remind yourself of the progress made more frequently and this in turn renews your hope. It's also important to really hold onto the fact that money is just one aspect of your true wealth. Friends, family and the memories you share are more precious than gold and while losing money may hurt, it doesn't even compare to having loved ones near.

We can easily convince ourselves that the more money we have the happier we are but that's just not true. There is not set amount that you will ever get to that provides true happiness. That is because happiness is an inside job and nothing external can change that. Hope in the future and faith in ourselves and our families are wonderful concepts that get us through these tough times.

I have dealt with many people who have occasionally suffered financial loss due to one circumstance or another and the interesting thing is that they are often the most grateful for what they have. They don't take wealth or security for granted and are very prudent with decisions in ways that others who have not learned these hard lessons aren't. Gratitude is a powerful emotion and can help you gain perspective in any situation especially when your future is at stake.

The Unexpected

Of course a good financial plan will help you prepare for unexpected events with insurance and other strategies, but often when we think about these events happening, we make faulty assumptions. For example, often we plan for insurance to cover the costs associated with something like a cancer diagnosis and of course it will. But we fail to take into account the emotional impact of this sort of thing. For example, I knew a relatively young CEO whose wife did get the unfortunate diagnosis of cancer. He had plenty of insurance, but he hadn't planned for the fact that he would completely drop out of his business for six months while she struggled to recover. People often make a financial plan on the assumption that if something like this happens, their income and other things in life will continue, and they will just have to worry about the medical expense but that's rarely a true assumption.

The emotional and physical toll that an unexpected health event has is devastating and may be drastically different from assumptions. There have been several instances where instead of living the retirement dream a couple had planned, one spouse has to put the other in a long term care facility. This completed changed the plan for their future.

One of the biggest dangers when an unexpected life event happens is to make rash decisions in the moment. There are many multi-layered items that must be considered. These include not only the present emergency, but also planning for the new directions and how that direction will impact the overall estate. It takes time to reconfigure an effective plan and doing things in a hurried, rash manner can cause a tremendous amount of disruption and deterioration of that nest egg.

There are several tools you can employ to help you get through trying personal and financial times in your life. These include:

1. Let it go – you cannot change events nor can you recreate something that is gone. Dwelling on what was just produces more negative emotions and prevents you from moving forward. Let the circumstance go and move on with 'what is'.

2. Understand yourself – know your own behavioral tendencies and put into place safeguards that will help you make good decisions rather than emotional ones in a time of distress. This may mean leaning on your financial team a little more or having another family member help you with the decision making process.

3. Create a new dream – life is all about change and your plan for the future may have done a 180 degree turn, but that doesn't mean it still can't be happy and fulfilling. You can choose to see the positive aspects in any circumstance even if it is just being grateful to have learned a hard lesson.

4. Take action – you still have a great deal to offer and will recover financially, but only if you make a new plan and take action on it. You can't wallow in despair. The only way to get to your new dream is to act with a new, but solid, plan in place.

There is no way to guess the future and I don't have a crystal ball any more than you do. What I can do is encourage your progress on the path to financial security. And even if you suffer some type of unexpected personal or financial loss, I can encourage your recovery as you regain that security once again.

While a good financial plan isn't insurance against all loss, it is a fortress of protection from most of the usual problems and life events that might arise.

Liars, Scoundrels and Thieves

Ever since the Bernie Madoff scandal, all investors, but especially those with a high net worth, have experienced a little uncertainty. Bernie Madoff created a Ponzi scheme in which people and even financial institutions invested in his fund and his 'proprietary trading strategies'. That money was then spent to line Madoff's own pockets. Investors still received very healthy returns at first, funded by the money provided by new investors, though their 'customized' statements showed it was their money growing – so they invested more. Eventually the house of cards Madoff built came crashing down and many investors, some of them very wealthy, were left on the verge of bankruptcy. It is estimated that the scam was in excess of $64 Billion.

You have to wonder, how is that even possible? How can one person bilk that many very sophisticated investors out of not only their life savings but their family's money that has been accumulated for generations? Yet we regularly hear of some hedge fund manager or financial maverick that bilked their customers out of millions. It is more widespread than even the media portrays and clearly, we are all at risk of falling prey to this type of scam no matter how smart or experienced an investor we think we are. It really bears talking about some of the warning signs and behaviors that got these particular investors into trouble and then developing some safeguards to put a padlock on your investments and ensure this doesn't happen to you.

In a perfect world, investors would behave rationally and take into account all information before making an informed and logical decision. But that's not what happens, in fact there is an entire field now called Behavioral Finance because often, rather than looking at facts, we invest with our emotions and crazy things happen because of it. This field of study looks at the reasons why we make sudden and seemingly irrational decisions with money and investments and will only grow.

We are more vulnerable to be taken advantage of financially because of a few underlying human tendencies. One is the idea that we are getting privileged or higher level investment information than anyone else. High net worth individuals are used to being offered unique and exclusive investment opportunities so when someone in a very well appointed office with a premium address offers you the chance to make a fortune, it sounds exciting. The person presenting the plan has years of experience and a supposedly impressive track record. All of a sudden you are convincing yourself to set aside that normal due diligence process and accept what is being offering because it sounds like you could make millions. In reality they are preying on your attraction to the idea that very few people are getting this offer and if you don't act now it will disappear.

We also put a lot more weight on recent events than past ones so when you are shown tremendous recent gains, the tendency is to believe those gains will continue. Now, reason would tell you that there are ups and downs and that big gains also can come with big losses so caution would seem to be prudent. But that's now how most people behave. They want to ride the wave of big returns and refuse to think about the fact that a market correction may be on the way.

We hold onto the memory of our gains and push the bad experience of loss way back in our minds. We want to believe the best but by doing so we expose our wealth to much greater risk than is warranted.

Greed is a bad word in most circles as it seems to denote a lack of control or consideration – and that is a good description. The idea that you could make some outlandish return very quickly gets that excitement building and so you invest a small amount to test it. When you are then presented a statement a very short while later showing the explosive growth of your money it is very hard not to want to sink more money into the investment and that is exactly how they draw you in. Once you realize you have been taken advantage of, it's very hard not to feel shame and embarrassment especially if you have some level of wealth. After all, shouldn't you know better?

Yes and no. Most people who have done some sort of financial planning have some structural protections in place to reduce conflicts of interest and ensure that the person giving advice is following some standard financial rules. But it's the behavioral issues that really trip us up especially when confronted with a con artist as experienced as Bernie Madoff. He used a combination of techniques not only to lure in wealthy clients but also to use their help to get even more investors.

I have dealt with very wealthy individuals for many years and even though most of them do have a certain level of sophistication concerning investments, they aren't professionals and their children and other family members certainly aren't. It's easy to assume because someone has money that they know everything about holding onto it, but it's just not true.

The words 'sophisticated investor' usually is connected to a high level of net worth and investing experience. It assumes a body of knowledge about money and investments but there is no standard for this term and includes various factors. This means that a spouse or second generation person, who may have known almost nothing about the family finances but is now in charge of a fortune, would be considered a sophisticated investor. This is the type of person that unscrupulous people try to take advantage of.

Most of the scandals we've read about lately come from unscrupulous individuals in the investing business, and not from well known, regulated companies. Investment advisors in these solid companies are held to much stricter rules and regulations and are required to offer advice that meets a 'fiduciary' standard. This means the advice offered should clearly be in the client's best interest if an outside third party looks at it. Their actions must fit a very narrow definition and this is a great protection for the client. They must also disclose any conflicts of interest which allow the client a better decision making process.

Due diligence is the key and keeping in mind the old adage, "If it sounds too good to be true, it probably is." Your financial future is nothing to gamble with and even if you make a mistake, you don't continue to throw good money after bad. Stop, reconsider and take another path.

Slow and Steady

This chapter has focused on the extreme circumstances that, other than death, many of us won't face for a very long time if ever. But it still bears addressing because they will happen to some. You shouldn't live in fear of what might happen, but you do need to be prudent and create a plan that covers most of the common scenarios. I know many older people who live almost in terror as they think their nest egg might evaporate but this is wasted energy. You have created a plan for a reason and that fear is simply a loss of the long vision perspective you once had.

The most important aspect of accomplishing your financial goals and dreams is holding on to perspective no matter where you are on the road to financial security right now. Remember, it's not a race. You don't win or lose, nor are you competing against anyone, you are just creating your own goals and dreams. Pace isn't relevant and your pace may be very different from your neighbors and that is okay.

It's common to think that you have to get all you can while things are hot and the market is rising, but that entails assuming more risk as well. As I often tell my clients, my favorite animal is the turtle. He's boring, consistent, and makes steady progress. Oh, I understand that he's not flashy or even interesting most of the time. In fact he's usually overlooked, but in the end that steady commitment gets him to the end goal, often way ahead of others who started off with excitement and pizzazz.

Financial progress and wealth accumulation are long term endeavors and even though we live in a fast paced, instant gratification world, money still works the same way it always has. The wonderful thing about growing money is that time works for you more so than large sums of money due the effect of compounding. Once this is really grasped especially by younger members of the family who will eventually inherit your hard earn money, then wealth accumulation can be passed on for generations.

Education is the real key to safeguarding your nest egg and passing it on. It is one of the things I strongly focus on. I encourage my clients to know as much as possible about their wealth accumulation and estate plan. Though some of the techniques and instruments used will be unfamiliar, it is always in your best interest to know as much as possible about what is going on with your money. I have numerous clients who would probably be happier if I just handled it and didn't explain everything so much, but that is not in their best interest.

There will be unexpected financial circumstances and trials that do arise over the years, but you can create a plan that allows for this variance and still ensure that you can weather almost any storm.

Chapter 10

The Real Goal is Peace of Mind

Chapter 10
The Real Goal is Peace of Mind

Peace of mind is a phrase that is flippantly uttered by many, but few ever really achieve their own personal peace of mind when it comes to their finances. Few would even list it as one of their financial goals, but it is the real underlying source of uncertainty for most people, which is a real shame. Fear can be easily kept at bay simply by implementing the right plan and keeping it solidly up to date each year. It sometimes feels easier just to avoid it altogether but in reality the opposite is true. By having something that you can look at and know you have thought through the various what ifs, and have in place your goals for the kind of lifestyle you want to live, it gives you comfort and security.

Growing wealth isn't just about you. It's also about those you leave behind whether they be family, charities, foundations and other entities that you want to benefit from your lifetime of work. While it can feel like you are carrying the weight of the world on your shoulders, it really comes down to thinking through the legacy you want to leave and then being sure you meet those goals.

The transference of wealth to loved ones is a major concern for those with substantial or even relatively modest estates and this is why so much of my time is spent on multigenerational education. It's time to face the fact that few people can or will teach their own children about money and that is extremely detrimental to their long term security. Learning about money and understanding how to sustain wealth doesn't just happen, it is learned and when knowledge is lacking then wealth is lost. We see all around us today a growing sense of entitlement to wealth. Many assume that just because they exist, they are deserving of the best life has to offer. What they overlook is the hard work, education and dedication that goes into creating wealth in the first place.

Recently we've seen on the news movements such as Occupy Wall Street that are an outward expression of this lack of understanding of financial issues. Rather than learn what it takes to create and sustain wealth, then spending a lifetime working toward those goals, it is easier to complain and blame someone else.

This movement is not a U.S. phenomenon either, almost every first world country is experiencing something similar and that is because they all have similar mindsets toward money. Entitlement is a multifaceted issue, but largely many first world countries including the U.S. have spent years handing out entitlements and people have come to see their government as a benefactor. Current U.S. government figures show that 47% of the population receives food stamps and more than 50% receive more in various benefits than they pay in taxes. This does not even make sense from a financial standpoint and it's clear that things have gone horribly wrong in society's attitude toward wealth.

There is a growing gap between the truly wealthy what was once the middle class. But the biggest gap isn't the actual dollars in the bank, it is in the financial attitudes and education that exist. Many have the idea that if someone has wealth they should want to share that wealth with others no matter the circumstances. The wealthy people I know are some of the most generous people I've ever met, but that doesn't mean they just fling money into the wind for anyone to grab. They put that money to work for the most good and that is not by supporting those who actively refuse to pay any attention to their own financial education.

Wealth must be something that is planned for and earned, it is not something anyone is entitled to, so the idea that somehow it is wrong to be wealthy is backward. The people who choose to educate themselves and plan for the future should not be punished for being financially responsible. One of the biggest causes of the current unrest is that many Baby Boomers never taught their children about money and many of them never learned themselves. It wasn't that they didn't care enough about their children; they actually cared too much. By that I mean that they wanted their children to have it easier than they did and have things they didn't have. So they gave it to them. When you give someone something they haven't earned, it sets up the expectation that is how the world works, and they come to expect it. How then can they ever understand how to work for something and how can they possibly teach the next generation? They can't. That means a large segment of the population has no idea how to even start to create and retain their own wealth and that is a fundamental problem. The current movements we are witnessing, such as Occupy Wall Street, are just an expression of frustration of this population base. Entitlements are not the answer, financial education is. If you want serious money, you have to get serious about money.

We live in a world where instant gratification is an expectation not just a possibility. We want what we want, and we want it NOW. This leads to questionable financial choices like the ones we have already discussed. The idea that you want to create wealth quickly opens you up to being scammed or investing in financial instruments that are way too risky in order to achieve your stated goals. Other people aren't' responsible for you getting yourself into a bad financial spot and the sooner you realize that the sooner you can take responsibility and start making changes.

Many people want to blame banks for the mortgage crisis, Wall Street for investment losses, and criminals for events such as the Bernie Madoff scandal. But think about these various issues for a moment and what they have in common. They would never occur if there weren't people who put their own greed above common sense. They wanted a bigger return than was reasonable or wanted to believe they could live in a bigger house than they could realistically afford. Greed drove them to set caution aside and not perform their own due diligence which set the stage for disaster. No one cares more about your future than you do and if you choose to set aside your own common sense, then don't expect that you won't suffer huge losses at some point.

The Biggest Issue

Most investors don't realize that they are their own worst enemy when it comes to growing their wealth over the long term. They turn on the news and hear that the financial sky is falling and panic, when most of the time the news they hear or read has nothing to do with their investments or long term strategy. Fear is terrible baggage to carry around and it's easy to think that as your wealth grows, that fear will dissipate. In reality for most people it is just the opposite – the more assets you accumulate the more fear you have of losing what you have worked your entire life for. Unfortunately fear often breeds avoidance behavior, meaning that the more an investor's fears grow the more reluctant they are to make or alter their financial plan because they are afraid they are worse off than they think and they'd rather not face the facts and just pretend everything is fine.

This is a warning sign. Are you putting off your own financial planning? Ask yourself why. Are you afraid you won't be worth as much as you thought? If so, then doesn't it make more sense to know that now so you can take steps to fix it? Maybe you think it will be a big hassle to round up all the paperwork not to mention the fact that you have to take the time to meet with an expert. I'll admit it does take some work to gather the paperwork, but most people spend much more time manicuring their lawn than they do focusing on growing their own wealth. When you think about it from that perspective it sounds a little silly. How can you justify not paying attention to your finances when how you live the rest of your life depends on it? Is that green grass really more important?

It is so very easy to set aside the important for the urgent – I even do it myself! But it will catch up with you so committing to the process is the first real step to taking control of your future and being sure you will meet your own goals. This also means tuning out all the bad financial news you hear or read each day. Honestly they never really talk about the good because that doesn't get near as good a ratings as it does for them to tell you how the financial system is teetering on the edge of ruin. Strange that's it's been 'teetering' for decades now! The truth is that your wealth isn't determined or affected by these broad generalizations because you have your own personal plan that is working for you. You also make minor adjustments to that plan each year to allow you to take full advantage of the changes in the market and avoid the pitfalls. This isn't taken on as a panicked knee jerk reaction to bad news, but is instead a carefully considered and thought out strategic plan that takes all the factors that are important to you into account.

There is a quote that first appeared in a Walt Kelley comic strip years ago. It says, "I have met the enemy and he is us!" That is especially true where our finances are concerned. We'd like to think it is external sources that are the cause of us not making millions from our investments, but the truth is that we are the cause. And if we are the cause then we are also the solution. It just takes education and discipline to grow your money into something you will be very proud of.

Not For the Faint of Heart

Creating and sustaining wealth is not easy. There are many things that can chip away at your plan if you are not vigilant. We all have preconceived ideas about how money works and sometimes these lead us to overlook some of the most insidious drains on our wealth. As I've discussed in previous chapters, the biggest of these drains is inflation. Most investors really underestimate the effect of inflation. In fact it's a word they hear so often that it carries little real meaning. We all know in a general sense that inflation erodes investment returns, but people don't think about the fact that inflation is really a double edged sword. Not only does it erode the returns an investor sees right now, it also diminishes future purchasing power and that is the real thief.

What if I told you that when you retire, you will be paying $20 for a gallon of milk? Sounds incredible doesn't it? But that is reality. In 1980, milk was about $1.50 per gallon, now it's closer to $5. Thirty years from now when you and I are in the midst of retirement, assuming average inflation, that same gallon will be $20. Investors often focus on today's inflation rate and understand that it cuts into their earnings, but they fail to think about the fact that the dollars they are making today will be worth much less when they retire and so they underestimate what it will actually take to live in retirement. A solid plan puts a virtual padlock on your wealth today and allows that wealth to produce a future with choices.

What they really want is peace of mind. It's not about having a particular amount of money stashed away for retirement, it is about being able to sleep at night and not worry about the future. Investors want to understand that what they have worked hard for is protected and also used to best position them for a future that has options. It can be unnerving to contemplate a future where your money might run out and you have few choices in how you live.

Investors also want to know that their wealth can be passed down and so I work very hard to assist entire families with multigenerational wealth plans. This ensures future generations will also benefit from their hard work and that includes a lot of financial education. Even very wealthy people often neglect to teach their children how to handle money so you commonly see a second generation quickly go through any inheritance they receive. I work hard with clients to ensure that wealth will be there to sustain the future of their families for the long term.

I've said many times, making money is the easy part, keeping it is the hard part. This is because things like inflation erode it constantly. It's like trying to pile ice cream on top of a cone on a hot summer day. The harder you work to add more ice cream, the faster it melts and so you must work even harder. That is exactly what it is like to grow your wealth – a constant uphill battle that will never end. You might even think of it like a bucket with a small hole in the bottom. As you are making money and earning more to add to your wealth, you don't really notice or think about that little hole. But then you retire and suddenly that bucket is emptying much faster than you anticipated and that is because that little hole (inflation) becomes more pronounced once you stop adding water to the bucket.

One of the biggest mistakes that investors make today is not having a good plan to compensate for inflation and other drains. But the second biggest is not keeping that plan up to date. Life circumstances, relationships and business interests change with surprising speed and for this reason you want to review your plan on no less than a yearly basis to ensure you are protecting your assets and growing them to their maximum advantage. I know that it's not the easiest thing in the world to think about creating a plan and in my case, when I work with a client, it's much more than just an average plan. I find it is essential to really talk to all the parties involved and get them thinking about what they really want. You can't imagine how many times one spouse has one idea of what retirement will look like, and their spouse has a completely different idea! By taking the time to talk through what you want life to look like down the road it gets everyone on the same page and working toward the same goals. It also helps everyone understand what has to happen to get there which produces better long term results.

That is not to say that investors don't worry about their money – they do. In fact some completely obsess about every little nuance. But this is largely because they are hypersensitive to risk. There is always risk and what the market is or isn't doing should not be their first concern. They must learn to balance risk with meeting their goals. Once they really understand their long term goals and have a plan to achieve them, the short term volatility of the market becomes a footnote. They realize that risk can be largely tamed through various investment strategies so the challenge then become balancing a reasonable amount of risk in order to meet the goals they say they want. If their goals and dreams are big, that may mean taking on more risk. If they are already well on their way to those goals, the strategy then becomes protecting what they have and continuing to grow their wealth in a steady fashion.

Wealth accumulation is a long term endeavor, not the lottery, but often investors treat it like the lottery. They try to pick an investment that will shoot up overnight and then stress over a downturn as if they are living on that money right now – but they aren't. They are in it for the long haul and over the long term the market will calm down and show steady growth and their investments will benefit from a calm and methodical approach.

The Real Deal

I have small children and I work hard even at their young ages to get them to understand how money works. I'm sure as they age I will expand their knowledge and education because I see it as one way I can ensure their future. Sure, I plan to work hard my entire life and hopefully leave them a little something. But whether I do or not, I know I will have already given them the best gift I could and that is knowledge. No amount of money will ever mean more than what I can teach them because without that instruction about money and how it works, wealth will always elude them.

Because I work with estate plans a great deal, I can't help but think about what I will leave behind for my family in terms of wealth. I've thought about it a lot and I know that it has nothing to do with cash or physical assets. Those things are good and meaningful on some level, but they are not the real wealth. Real wealth is an understanding of the value of family, friends and life experiences. It is the appreciation of a beautiful sunrise and the joy of a quiet morning run alongside a centuries old European castle. Wealth gives the opportunity to have these experiences, but it is the experience that is the journey, not merely the accumulation of money. It is this type of understanding that I will leave behind. Money gives you choices in life, but it is merely a tool; an instrument of dream fulfillment and conveyance for peace of mind. Not the peace of mind that more 'stuff' brings, but the kind where you know you will be provided for and able to live in comfort.

This is exactly why I love what I do so much. I have the opportunity every day to positively affect the lives of my clients', their children and their children's children which will allow them to reach their goals and live a life of opportunity and rich experiences. We all learn through experiences whether they are good or bad. They shape who we are and they determine if we have a life well lived.

We all know people that we look at and say, "You know he/she really lived!" For me, this means that they approached life with joy and eagerness in search of the next experience that would allow them to experience even more joy. They didn't sit back and accept the status quo, instead they jumped up and ran to meet all that life had in store for them. Many people allow fear to drag them down and suck all the joy from what they could be experiencing right now. This fear stems from worry and much of that worry is financial. They spend so much time agonizing over questionable financial moves in the past or worrying about the future that they completely miss the wonderful experiences of today.

If there is any encouragement that I can leave you with, it's not to sacrifice today worrying about yesterday or tomorrow. If you've made mistakes, let them go and commit to getting on a clear path to financial freedom. If you have accumulated some wealth and now fear that it might evaporate into some unknown void, now is the time to set a plan in place to release that worry. There is so much more to this life than financial worry and you have the ability to free yourself from that worry and at the same time set a clear path to increasing your wealth over the long term. Every day you wait is another day wasted and you can never get it back. Choose today to set your plan in motion so you can experience all that life has for you.

Glossary

Glossary

A

Asset Allocation - the strategy behind an investor's decision to construct an investment portfolio in a certain way. Stocks, bonds, and cash (short-term investments) are the three principal asset classes or investment types used in asset allocation.

Average Term to Maturity - each bond in a bond/fund portfolio has a specific amount of time between now and when it matures. The average term to maturity is the arithmetic average length of time until the average bond in a fund/portfolio will mature or be redeemed by its issuer.

B

Bankers' Acceptance - a money market instrument issued by a non-financial corporation but guaranteed as to principal and interest by its bank. The guarantee results in a higher issue price and consequent lower cost to the issuer.

Basis Point - 1/100 of one percent. A 0.5% change in interest rates is referred to as a change of 50 basis points.

Bear Market - a period of sustained declining market prices.

Benchmark Portfolio - the personalized asset allocation that has been selected as the primary strategy to meet each client's objectives. This portfolio is developed jointly by the client and a team of advisors. Portfolio action will deviate from this "neutral" position when the investment management team deems it appropriate.

Bull Market - a period of sustained rising market prices.

C

Central Bank - in Canada, the Bank of Canada; in the U.S., the Federal Reserve Board. The central bank is responsible for setting short-term interest rates (the Bank rate in Canada; the discount rate in the U.S.). These rates are an important tool in implementing monetary policy, by which the central banks seek to ensure that the economy grows in a sustainable fashion and inflationary pressures are contained.

Charitable Remainder Trust - A trust that pays an income to one or more individuals for a specified length of time then leaves the remainder of the trust to a designated charity. A charitable remainder trust can produce substantial tax benefits and is particularly suitable for use by a married couple with no children.

Credit Rating - the ability of an issuer to repay its level of debt on a relative basis, as assessed by an independent rating agency. The Government of Canada has the highest-ranked credit quality in Canada.

Currencies - international investing means buying: (a) a foreign security and, as a result; (b) the currency in which that security is denominated. Portfolio managers either filter out (hedge), actively manage, or seek foreign currency exposure depending on the expected trend in value for the investor's home currency relative to the foreign currency.

D

Defensive Sectors - areas of the equity market, such as utilities and health care stocks, that are favored by investors as a safe haven during times of uncertainty or extreme volatility. These stocks are defensive by nature as they typically offer predictable earnings growth and reliable dividend payments in both good and bad economies.

Derivatives - index futures and options that reflect the price movement of an underlying security (e.g., a stock market index), but are traded separately from the cash market.

Discretionary Portfolio - once an investment strategy is agreed upon by a client and a portfolio manager, the portfolio manager is given the discretion to oversee the account's administration and adjust portfolio holdings when opportunities and market conditions warrant.

E

Emerging Markets - developing countries with relatively low per capita income, often with above-average economic growth potential.

Equity or Shareholders' Equity - ownership interest of common and preferred stockholders in a company. Also, the difference between the assets and liabilities of a company, sometimes called net worth.

F

Fiscal Policy - a key responsibility of the federal and provincial governments, which involves preparing the budget and financial strategy for the country or province. Among the tools of fiscal policy are taxation and government payments.

Fixed Income Securities - securities that generate a defined set of payments, such as interest or dividend income, including bonds, debentures and preferred shares.

Fundamentals - refer to relevant factors or data that influence the value of a particular security, such as a company's stock or a country's currency. In the case of a stock, for example, the company's sales, earnings, debt and dividend prospects are fundamentals that would affect share price. Similarly, a country's economic growth rate, interest rate policy and trade patterns are factors that potentially influence the strength or weakness of its currency.

G

Gross Domestic Product (GDP) Growth - GDP is the value of total production of goods and services in a country over a specified period, typically a year. How much GDP grows from one period to the next is an indication of a country's economic health.

Growth Stock - stocks whose revenues and/or earnings are growing faster than the average company at the current time.

H

Hard Landing - falls somewhere between a soft landing and a recession. That is, an economic slowdown to 1% to 2% growth, which is good for containing inflation but teeters on the edge of recession.

Hedge Fund - a broad category of portfolio, or fund, that seeks to reduce risk by transferring some of that risk to another investor. These types of assets will generally have a low correlation with equity or bond markets.

Henson Trust - A Henson trust (sometimes called an absolute discretionary trust), in Canadian law, is a type of trust designed to benefit disabled persons. Specifically, it protects the assets (typically an inheritance) of the disabled person, as well as the right to collect government benefits and entitlements.

I

Index - e.g., the S&P/TSX Composite Index or the S&P 500 Index (U.S.). A leading benchmark of equity or bond performance which is used to answer the question, "What did the market do today?" An index is typically composed of several industry sectors.

Index Futures - a stock index future is an agreement to take, or make, delivery of an amount of cash determined by the difference between the level of the specified stock index at the time you enter into the contract and the level of the index at the time you exit the contract. This investment approach allows the investor to take advantage of changes in the index, without actually buying the individual securities which make up the index.

Inflation - Inflation is defined as a sustained increase in the general level of prices for goods and services. It is measured as an annual percentage increase. As inflation rises, every dollar you own buys a smaller percentage of a good or service. There are three variations of inflation:

- Deflation is when the general level of prices is falling. This is the opposite of inflation.
- Hyperinflation is unusually rapid inflation. In extreme cases, this can lead to the breakdown of a nation's monetary system. One of the most notable examples of hyperinflation occurred in Germany in 1923, when prices rose 2,500% in one month!
- Stagflation is the combination of high unemployment and economic stagnation with inflation. This happened in industrialized countries during the 1970s, when a bad economy was combined with rising oil prices

Inter Vivos Trust – A trust set up during the settlor's lifetime. *Inter vivos* is Latin for "among the living".

L

Liquidity - the ability to turn your investment into cash immediately. Alternatively, the flow of cash into and out of markets, whether domestic or international, which can affect interest rates and corporate profits.

M

Market Capitalization - the aggregate market value of a security, calculated by multiplying the current price per share by the total number of shares issued.

Market Sectors - interest-sensitives, e.g. utilities, real estate, financial services and pipelines, are especially affected by changes in interest rates. Cyclicals, e.g. steel, industrial companies, autos, etc., are sensitive to the business cycle. Resources, e.g. mines, gold, oil and gas and forestry products, are sensitive to commodity prices.

Monetary Policy - a policy often implemented by a central bank to control credit and the money supply in the economy, in an attempt to control inflation and stimulate or slow an economy.

One tool of monetary policy is the setting of short-term interest rates.

P

Peace of Mind - The absence of mental stress or anxiety, and the presence of serenity, calm, quiet, comfort of mind; inner peace.

Portfolio Manager - each Private Investment Counsel portfolio is overseen by a dedicated Portfolio Manager, an accredited investment professional. The Portfolio Manager begins with a series of discussions with the client, leading to a highly personalized investment strategy.

Proprietary Pooled Portfolio - a portfolio comprised of managed investment funds (pooled funds) that have low or no management fees embedded in the funds. Pooled funds are typically held by individuals or institutions investing larger sums.

R

Recession - technically defined as at least two consecutive quarters when the economy shrinks or fails to grow.

S

Segregated Portfolio - an investment portfolio of individual stocks and bonds.

Small-, Mid-, Large-Capitalization - reflects the size and dollar value of the companies whose securities are listed on the exchanges. Capitalization is often shortened to "cap" in this context. Small-cap stocks are usually less liquid (harder to buy and sell) than large-caps. Bank stocks are large-cap. Many high-tech stocks are small-cap.

Soft Landing - a moderate slowing of economic growth to a rate of about 2% to 3%, which is expected to keep inflation from accelerating.

Spread - commonly used to describe the difference in yield between short- and long-term bonds or between Canadian and U.S. bonds of similar term to maturity. Could also be the difference between the bid and asking prices of a stock or bond.

Supranational Organizations - a world or regional organization that is not tied to any one sovereign country, such as the World Bank, which issues bonds to finance its activities.

Systematic Risk – is the variability of returns that is due to macroeconomic factors that affect all risk assets. It cannot be eliminated through diversification.

T

Total Rate of Return - the percentage change in the total value of an investment portfolio including interest income, dividends paid on equities, and the change in market value of the portfolio over a specified time period. The calculation will include both realized and unrealized capital changes, and it may be calculated and expressed as a return that is net of expenses and/or taxes. Often expressed as the annual compound rate.

Testamentary Trust – A trust created by the settlor's will which is invoked upon death.

Trust – A trust is a legal arrangement whereby one or more persons (trustees) hold legal title to property (trust property) for the benefit of other persons (beneficiaries). The person who creates the trust and puts ("settles") property into it is called the settler.

U

Underweight and Overweight - refers to deviations in the neutral asset allocation of a benchmark portfolio, underweight being less than the neutral, overweight more. For example, the benchmark neutral asset allocation for a balanced portfolio might typically be 60% in equities, 30% in bonds, and 10% in cash. If the asset mix is shifted to reflect a 50% position in equities, 40% exposure to bonds and a 10% holding in cash, the portfolio would be underweight equities, overweight bonds and neutral cash.

Unit Trusts - a mutual fund structure which allows funds to hold assets and pass investment returns through to the individual owners of the trust units.

Unsystematic Risk – risk that is unique to an asset, derived from its particular characteristics. It can be eliminated in a diversified portfolio.

Y

Yield - an ambiguous term having several possible meanings:

a. *Current yield*: annualized interest income on a bond expressed as a percentage of its current market value.

b. *Dividend yield*: same as current yield, but applied to dividend income on a stock's price.

c. *Yield-to-maturity*: the annualized total return, expressed as a percentage that a bond will provide to the investor if held to its final maturity date.

Yield Curve - the relationship among the yields to maturity of bonds (usually government bonds) of the same quality but different maturities, ranging from 30 days to 30 years, put into graphic form.